Cars of the World in Colour

PASSENGER CARS
1913–23

by
T. R. NICHOLSON

Illustrated by
JOHN W. WOOD

Norman Dinnage
Frank Friend
Brian Hiley
William Hobson
Tony Mitchell
Jack Pelling

LONDON
BLANDFORD PRESS

First published in 1972
© 1972 Blandford Press Ltd
167 High Holborn, London WC1V 6PH
ISBN 0 7137 0574 4

Colour section printed by Colour Reproductions Ltd, Billericay
Printed and bound by
Richard Clay (The Chaucer Press) Ltd, Bungay, Suffolk

INTRODUCTION

The ten years between 1913 and 1923 were dominated by a World War in which a generation came to grips with the internal-combustion engine, on land, on sea, and in the air. The result was a social revolution. Yet it would be fair to say that its effect upon the automobile was more one of accelerated evolution.

Already in 1913 better-to-do motorists could have most of the refinements normally associated with the 1920s—electric lighting and starting, quick-detachable wheels, and closed coachwork. Mass production had been with us since Henry Ford opened his first moving assembly line in 1913, and even before the outbreak of war the seeds had been sown of that American domination of world export markets that was to last until 1941.

Further, American continuity of production during the War meant steadily increasing outputs, with only a brief pause in 1917 and 1918, though like most American trends this one was not destined to hit Europe until several years later. Even in 1914, deliveries of three thousand passenger cars in a twelve-month period were beyond the capacity of the average European factory, though firms of the calibre of FIAT, Peugeot, and Wolseley could and did achieve such levels. Not that they did so by methods that would have been acceptable in Detroit: their automobiles were the work of craftsmen, bearings were still scraped in by hand, and bodywork usually entrusted to outside firms. Many a smaller factory subsisted on assembly of other people's bits and pieces, but it was still possible for a tiny regional concern to be self-contained and make a profit on 50–80 units a year: a classic instance was the engineering works in a Somerset village responsible for the Mendip (22).

By contrast, America was geared to volume production. In 1916 at least fifteen companies could claim outputs of over ten thousand cars a year, and these included Cadillac, whose recently-introduced vee-eight was a $2,100 (£420) item. Thus by the Armistice the minimum number of cars which a small manufacturer could market economically in a calendar year was around two thousand, and thus concerns like Apperson (44) were doomed, excellent though their 'manufactured' 'Eight With Eighty Less Parts' might be. Bought-out components began to intrude, and by 1926 their handsome Lycoming-powered straight-eight stood no chance against competitors such as Hupmobile, who offered the same virtues for less money, and could afford a better dealer coverage.

Europe was already aware of the American menace. Though it took a war to reconcile Europeans to the ugliness and crude workmanship of the cheap American car, Giovanni Agnelli of FIAT was warning against the low cost-per-copy figures achieved by Detroit, and W. R. Morris took the view that 'if you can't beat 'em, join 'em', his 1915 Cowley (36) being an assembly of American-built mechanical elements.

The post-Armistice situation, of course, was uncomfortably different. A potential market triple the size of

1914's wanted more cars, cheaper cars, and all the refinements you could buy in America for under a thousand dollars, which meant full electrics. André

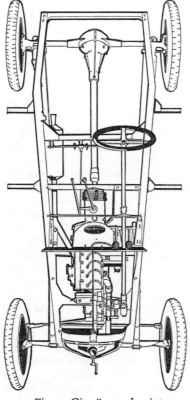

Fig. 1. Citroën 5c chassis

Citroën introduced flow-production to France in 1919, and by 1923 Renault (68), FIAT (79), and Morris were turning out inexpensive models in quantities hitherto unprecedented—twenty thousand a year and more. Sometimes the plan backfired. Marius Berliet sought to combine American methods

and an American type of car with his VB-type (54), and landed himself in receivership, while Emile Mathis (40) was under-capitalised, and his firm was one of the first to sink in the Great Depression of 1929–32.

The European middle-class manufacturer, by contrast, rode out the early 1920s with impunity, though the writing was on the wall. Typical of these were Star of Great Britain (58) and De Dion-Bouton of France (55). Their conservative clienteles were still content with slightly up-dated versions of 1914 themes, which meant electric starters, detachable cylinder heads, and the deletion of the transmission brake. Unfortunately such companies lacked the financial resources to branch out into any new departures, while even had they raised the money, their antiquated factories could never have coped with the outputs necessary to keep prices down to economic levels. They might still be good for a thousand cars a year in 1923, but within seven years organisations of the stamp of Vermorel (6) would have faded away.

Even in 1913, of course, the automobile had long since passed out of the experimental stage, and only in the realms of brakes and tyres was that year's best inferior to its 1923 counterpart. Cadillac had standardised electric lighting and starting in 1912, followed in the next two years by almost the entire American industry: Hudson (1) had them by 1913, and only the cheapest models, such as Ford and Saxon (2) held out. In Europe Hispano-Suiza and Lancia (28) led the way with full electrics. Four-wheel brakes had been available on three makes—Arrol-Johnston, Crossley, and Isotta Fraschini

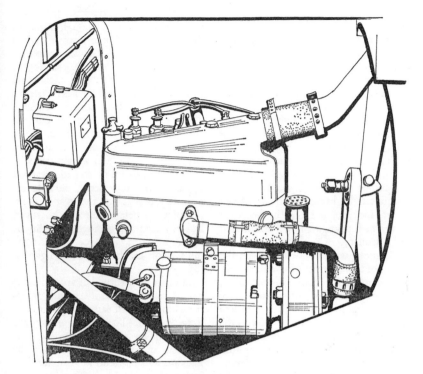

Fig. 2. De Dion-Bouton

(27) as early as 1910, even if neither British firm had persevered with them. Full-pressure lubrication was widely used, even if by no means universal; American firms were to persist with splash systems for a long while to come. The quick-detachable wheel had been pioneered by Rudge-Whitworth in 1907, and a whole host of proprietary types were on the market by 1914, notably the American Houk and the British Riley, used by several foreign makers such as Züst (14). Humber, Renault, and Fischer (16) made their own.

European and American strains, which had converged in 1904 with cars like the early four-cylinder Packards and Locomobiles, diverged again. The average European family model of 1913–14 was exemplified by the 12–20 h.p. La Buire (4). Power units tended to have four water-cooled cylinders cast monobloc, since Europe had rapidly become disenchanted with the six, thanks to its appalling vibration periods, and though Lanchester's vibration damper had rectified this fault, such units were now reserved for luxury carriages. Side valves in a L-head had largely supplanted the earlier T-head configuration with its two side camshafts, though some conservative firms like Vermorel adhered to the latter. High-tension magneto ignition was virtually universal, though more expensive cars had a standby coil. Unit gearboxes were gaining in fashion and the fabric- or leather-faced cone clutch was being supplanted by the smoother plate types. Non-detachable heads were still the order of the day, and the now ubiquitous oil dipstick was a seldom-encountered luxury—when Owen Clegg incorporated one in his 1912 Rover 12 h.p. engine it was considered revolutionary.

Opinions were divided between the merits of three and four forward speeds, as few motorists 'drove on the gear', while an undesirable cost-cutting device was the transaxle, found on cars like the A.C. (7). Almost universal was the combination of selective gate change with right-hand control, exceptions being the Renault and the minimal Humberette (10), which retained the awkward progressive quandrant. Also common to most cars was the use of semi-elliptic leaf springs at front and rear, though heavier models such as Rolls-Royce (50) and Lanchester favoured cantilevers at the back for their excellent ride and freedom from body roll, and in countries with bad roads, such as Sweden, there was a vogue for three-quarter elliptics, found on the Scania-Vabis (29) and on comparable German cars exported to Scandinavia and Central Europe.

Shaft drive was universal, with the honours divided between bevel and worm. Chain transmissions were reserved for cyclecars and the heaviest sporting machinery, though some of the traditionalists, like Isotta Fraschini and FIAT, offered it as an option on certain models. Only Argyll (1911) followed the pioneers with anchors on all four wheels, which makes their 1914 bankruptcy all the more lamentable. The 15–30 h.p. (8) had an efficient coupled system. Others adhered to traditional methods of retardation: a large, fade-prone, and sometimes self-incandescent drum behind the gearbox operated by the pedal, and lever-operated brakes on the rear wheels. Daimler and Peugeot already, however, had reversed the arrangements in the modern idiom, and so, surprisingly, did Calcott on their 10·5 h.p. light car (9).

Engines now turned at around 2,000 r.p.m., anything more being exceptional in an era of cast-iron pistons and long strokes. The alloy piston was already being used on sporting machinery, and was to be taken up by Packard and Franklin in America during the War. An 'average' $2\frac{1}{2}$-litre family-car unit developed some 30–35 b.h.p., sufficient to propel it at 50 m.p.h., with a cruising gait of around 35–40.

Technical thought was, however, turning towards substitutes for the poppet-valve. Charles Yale Knight's double-sleeve valves had been adopted by Daimler and Minerva in 1909, and other users were Russell of Canada (31) and the American Brewster (32). The Burt single-sleeve-valve, an Argyll preserve, was also found in the Swiss Piccard-Pictet (43), and other oddities were the rotary valves of certain Darracq and Itala models, and the Swiss Martin Fischer's crescent valve

(16). All were undoubtedly quieter than contemporary units of orthodox type, with such honourable exceptions as the Rolls-Royce, but all posed problems of lubrication, seizures being catastrophic events. They were also expensive to make, and the Knight, if America thought differently. Bad roads called for soft suspensions, while a public both untechnical and automobile-oriented demanded that the vehicle should be easy to drive and to maintain. Hence the rise of the cheaper coil ignition, which produced a better

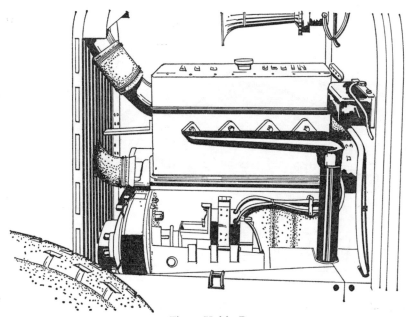

Fig. 3. Voisin R4

not the Burt, was adept at laying its own smokescreen. Towards the end of our period, some of the better ones, notably the Voisin (56) and the Peugeot, were becoming quite efficient, and rotating at a terrifying 4,000 r.p.m., but the trend was doomed once cheaper methods of sound-damping became general practice in the early 1930s.

Such was the European idiom. spark at low revolutions and helped flexibility. Hence also a greater standardisation of design. Not only were American cars built to a 'standard tread' (track) of fifty-six inches: they almost invariably had side-valve monobloc engines, three-speed unit gearboxes (though the transaxle was favoured by Studebaker), and all brakes on the rear wheels. Engines were big, lazy, and flexible; the admirable

Dodge (33) gave a paltry 25 b.h.p. from three-and-a-half litres. Detachable wheels were usually available only as a high-cost option, except on luxury models and on sporty types like the Templar (64); the fixed wood wheel with its quick-demountable rim was brake levers, to allow easy access from either side, and this permitted something seldom encountered in Europe until the middle 1920s, a four-seater body with four doors.

Multi-cylinderism also bulked larger. This was partly due to an endemic

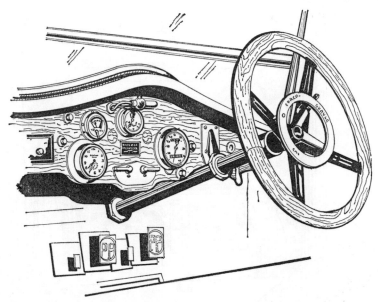

Fig. 4. Pic-Pic cockpit

considered easier for American womanhood to handle, and this feeling continued until 1931.

Controls were likewise different. Despite a right-hand rule of the road, left-hand steering had not been adopted by Ford until 1908, but by 1915 the rest of the industry had followed suit, only Pierce-Arrow (34) holding out until 1920, as befitted a chauffeur-driven carriage. With left-hand drive came the central location of gear and dislike for shifting gears, which called for greater flexibility, but the acceptance of the six was undoubtedly accelerated by the big production runs which made inexpensive multi-cylinderism economically viable. In 1913, for instance, Buick (37) made only fours, having but recently discarded the double-opposed twins on which their reputation had been founded. Their first six-cylinder cars came in 1914, and two years later they dropped their inexpensive four-cylinder line in favour of a 'Light Six' of under four litres capacity. In the same year Saxon came out with a 2·9-litre six, and at the end of our period Essex (46) replaced their successful four with a tiny 2·1-litre six-cylinder type. Though four-cylinder automobiles still dominated the lower echelons of the market—among 1923's crop were Chevrolet, Dodge, Durant, Gray, Hupmobile, Maxwell, Nash (72), and Overland, as well as the ubiquitous Ford (47), multi-cylinderism marched on. 1915 saw Cadillac's vee-eight, and a year later there were more modest offerings from Apperson, Briscoe, Oakland, and Oldsmobile, among others. Casting problems were to keep the vee engine out of the bargain-basement class until 1932, but it retained its following in a higher price category, as witness Cole, Lincoln, Peerless, and Wills-Sainte Claire (65).

Straight-eights had still to gain widespread acceptance, neither the Duesenberg (63) nor Britain's Leyland (57) being made in appreciable quantities, though in 1916 Packard marketed the world's first commercially-produced vee-twelve (35), which sparked off a small wave of imitators, aided and abetted by a proprietary unit of this type made by Weidely. The real vogue of the Twelve was, however, to be a phenomenon of the late 1920s and early 1930s. Like that other aid to smoothness, the sleeve-valve, it was to succumb to more sophisticated techniques.

The period saw the evolution of the modern small car as it was understood until the Volkswagen–Mini era. Before 1912, the smallest vehicles tended to have one or two cylinders; pint-sized

fours were too expensive to make, and suffered from abysmal power-to-weight ratios. From 1913 onwards we can see the evolution of the true big-car in miniature, using a four-cylinder engine, a sliding-type gearbox, and bevel or worm drive. The result was easily manageable by the distaff side, and was capable of around 40 m.p.h. Typical examples are the British A.C. (7), Calcott (9), and Standard (11), and the German Adler (23) and Wanderer (26). Provided no attempt was made to carry more than two passengers, they were respectable performers, the Adler attaining 50 m.p.h. Generally speaking, engines of 1,100–1,300 c.c. were used, though the Calcott was rather bigger, and the Bugatti-designed 'Bébé' Peugeot (5) made do on 856 c.c. German makers favoured tandem seating, while such lightweights gained little support in America, the Saxon (2) apart. The Trumbull (20) sold mainly abroad.

Alongside such 'real' cars, the cyclecar pursued its meteoric course. Born of the gutlessness of earlier lightweights, it was doomed from the moment that Morris, Singer, and A.C. offered new standards for less than £200 ($1,000), even if that legendary cyclecar-killer, the Austin Seven, did not appear until 1922. The cyclecar theme was the reverse of Henry Ford's principle of offering the most for the least money, for the hole-and-corner manufacturers in their back-street workshops vied with each other to offer the minimum that could be unloaded on a gullible customer. The vee-twin engines and belt drive of such devices as the Imp (18) were allied to such barbarities as cable-and-bobbin steering of non-Ackermann type, and

9

plywood construction. A post-War car shortage prolonged the agony until 1921, since the only sort of automobile that a Briton could buy for £100 was the Carden (49). Even the air-cooled

that conferred a legal status on the breed. The results were unexpected and not at all what the sponsors desired. On the one hand there were impossible eccentricities like the Cyclauto (66);

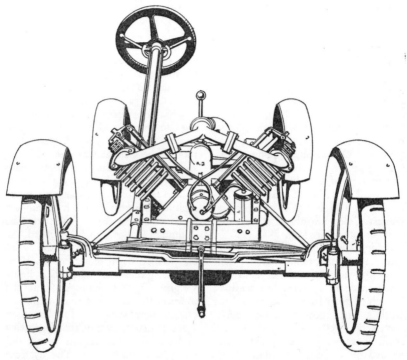

Fig. 5. Buckingham chassis

Rover Eight, with its noisy engine and hand starting, cost £300. The cyclecar vogue was non-existent in Italy, where there were no marginal motorists anyway, and brief in America, where long distances and poor roads allowed no scope for development. By contrast it lingered on until 1925 in France, thanks to a well-meaning government

on the other hand firms like Salmson and Amilcar evolved their 'cyclecars' into ferocious little two-seater sports models eminently unsuited to quiverful Duponts. It was left to Citroën (73) and Renault (68) to make proper light cars.

A few makers, notably Humber (10) and Swift (12) in England, opted for a half-way house in which a simple twin-cylinder engine was wedded to a car-type transmission and chassis. This saved about £50 on the purchase price, but the inherent roughness of these power units made them at best an interim type, and though the popular Rover sold briskly between 1921 and

motorist certainly could not, and the average model he could buy was still warmed-over 1914, like the 10/30 PS Bergmann-Métallurgique (24). Many designers and manufacturers had, however, had aero-engine experience in the 1914–18 period, learning to work with

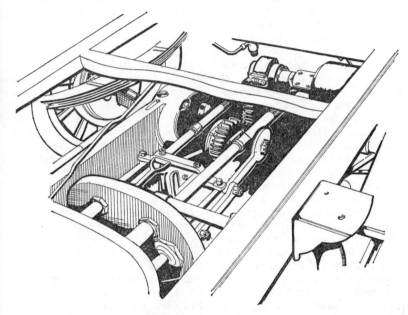

Fig. 6. Stanley engine

1925, Armstrong Siddeley's Stoneleigh (69), a late contender, was virtually stillborn. Who wanted such crude devices when a 5CV Citroën cost no more, even with import duty added?

If the War's main consequences were social and economic, new techniques and new materials appeared upon the automotive scene. Not that everyone was to benefit from these in our period: the average German

light alloys, and sampling the brilliant design of Marc Birkigt's vee-eight Hispano-Suiza. This was to become the ancestor of the classic M.G.s of the 1930s, but ten years earlier the wealthy could profit by the sophistication of Parry Thomas's Leyland Eight (57), Rowledge's 40–50 Napier (76), the Lanchester Forty (42), and the Wills-Sainte Claire (65). All featured overhead camshafts, and light alloys figured prominently in their specifications, if not perhaps as extensively as in the more modest German Audi 14/50 (78), which boasted an alloy block, pistons, and rear axle casing. None of these, of course, was cheap to make, and once the euphoria of 1919 faded into the strikes and lock-outs of 1920-21, sales dwindled before many a new luxury project could reach the public. FIAT, for instance, hurriedly shelved their twelve-cylinder super-car in order to concentrate on the 'safe' 1½-litre 501 (79) for the popular market. Americans might admire the avant-garde Duesenberg, but what they bought were the more staid Cadillacs, Lincolns, and Pierce-Arrows. Napier and Leyland abandoned passenger cars, Wills fled, too late, to the haven of a simpler six-cylinder machine, and Lanchester backed his Forty with a more modest Twenty-One. In the midst of all this technical brouhaha the Rolls-Royce (50) from the Class of '06 went on selling majestically to a clientele which knew nothing of light alloys, and only cared about what a car did, and how it did it.

Already, too, the wartime influences were making themselves felt. In 1915 Morris had shown that a 1,500 c.c. engine sufficed for a family four-seater, and by the early 1920s the German Aga (51) and the Italian O.M. (70) showed a widespread acceptance of this theme: the O.M. even had four-wheel brakes. These were conventional side-valvers, but Wolseley were cashing in on their Hispano experience with a 1,261 c.c. o.h.c. '10·5', and in Italy Ansaldo (52) offered a cheap car built in their former aero-engine works. It failed only because FIAT were in an unassailable position; what is more,

they were just as well versed in the new techniques which were already being exploited on their racers. By the end of 1924 they would be ready with their 990 c.c. 509, a really cheap baby car with both an upstairs camshaft and brakes on all the wheels.

Bodies made tremendous strides. In 1914 only the biggest firms—and those with advanced and cohesive thinking like Lanchester—made their own coachwork, and even then this was largely bespoke. Standardisation in this field was an American preserve. The big breakthrough, however, came in 1914, when Budd of Philadelphia evolved the new art of presswork. Their all-steel welded and riveted bodies were adopted by Dodge, and suddenly a combination of long runs and low prices became viable. Furthermore, the new method accelerated the development of 'stream line', giving a smooth continuity of line from radiator cap to rear seats. Gone was that untidy up-sweep on the firewall where a coach-builder sought to match his creation to the line of the chassis maker's hood. Renault's coal-scuttle style with dashboard radiator presented few problems, but the round hoods of such breeds as the Delaunay-Belleville or the early Franklin could produce some appalling dissonances. A comparison of style between the 1913 Hudson (1) or 1914 Maxwell (19) and the 1918 Buick (37) shows how rapidly this process evolved.

With Budd's discoveries came the prospect of light and inexpensive closed bodies. Before 1914, most closed cars were either formal limousines and landaulettes, or two-seater coupés of the type traditionally associated with physicians. Some, like the 1913 Bébé Peugeot (5) possessed a baroque elegance, but they were top-heavy and expensive, while a combination of weight and drag played havoc with an already limited performance. Even in America, sedans cost twice as much as tourings in 1918–19. As for Europe, problems of sound-damping rendered small closed vehicles scarcely habitable: the friction-driven G.W.K. (21) eventually died because of the inherent resonances of its transmission. It was not until 1925 that Citroën brought Budd's methods across the Atlantic, but by this time the sedan was firmly established in America, thanks to the Essex coach of 1922 (46) which was hardly heavier than a touring car and cost only $100 more.

If full electrics and coil ignition had been with us before the War, four-wheel brakes as general practice were a post-Armistice phenomenon. Of the pre-War systems, only Argyll's had been really efficient, but 1919 saw Marc Birkigt's brilliant Hispano-Suiza servo, other luxury cars to feature brakes on all wheels being the CO-type Delage and Cattaneo's straight-eight Isotta Fraschini. All these machines, of course, used the coupled type, and by 1923 such makers as Darracq (47) and Voisin (56) had followed suit. Duesenberg's hydraulics, understandably, took longer to catch on, though by 1924 fifteen American makers (Case, Chrysler, Davis, DuPont, Elcar, Flint, Hupmobile, Jordan, Kissell, McFarlan, Paige, Peerless, Velie, Westcott, and Wills-Sainte Claire) had them. Britain was more conservative, probably because experience with the original uncoupled type had shown that the

need to apply both pedal and lever in an emergency defeated the object of the exercise.

With four-wheel brakes came the low-pressure tyre, running at 16 psi instead of the traditional 60 psi. This made for a softer ride and longer tyre life, though until chassis were redesigned to meet the new fashion, heavy steering and greater running resistance were the order of the day, while motorists found wheel-wobble an uncomfortable substitute for the 'dreaded side-slip'. These improvements, however, deterred anyone from following Leslie Hounsfield's solution—cantilever suspension and solid tyres on his 1923 Trojan utility. (77).

Heterodoxy was on its way out. The attempts of Rumpler (59) and Leyat (74) to apply aeroplane techniques beyond the realm of engine design were met with blank stares. Steam reached its apotheosis in the Doble (71) of 1923, which could compete with the best that the gasoline engine could do, but it was murderously expensive, and it had come too late, eleven years after the advent of the electric self-starter. It had also come to the wrong country, for the United States were irrevocably committed to the internal combustion engine. Electricity, likewise, had outlasted its usefulness as the motive power for passenger automobiles, though curiously enough America was the type's last stronghold, with the Detroit (17) and the Rauch and Lang still listed as late as 1925. The former indeed soldiered on as a pale shadow of its former self until Pearl Harbour. It had, however, little chance against the gasoline automobile in 1914, and none at all

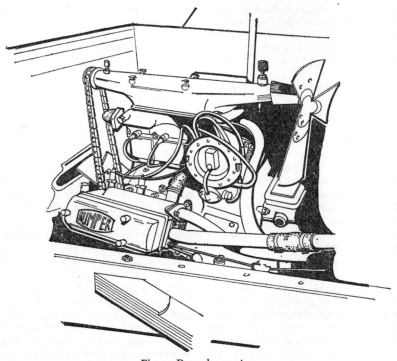

Fig. 7. Rumpler engine

once the twin weapons of the advertising agent and the stylist were unleashed on the car-owning public in the 1920s. Batteries were, as ever, the basic limitation, while even a wealthy family saw no point in maintaining an archaic-looking brougham at the town house, when a Packard Eight could waft them in equal comfort through city streets and rural highways.

As to the international picture, it was America all the way, though France and Italy shared the small-car honours, and in non-manufacturing countries like Portugal Citroën and Renault fought a ding-dong battle against FIAT. The Americans were unafraid of tariffs, and by the end of our period they had established assembly plants in Belgium, and even in Japan, where the Lila (80) was a feeble representative of a weakly, nascent industry which a recent writer has summarised as a 'long and hesitant sunrise'. Detroit lost out only where import duties were accompanied, as in Britain, by a horse-power tax favouring small-bore engines. This made the Model-T subject to an annual impost of £23, even if the substantial British content of Manchester-assembled examples allowed Ford to sell it at £110 in 1924. When 'Lizzie' finally gave way to the conventional Model-A in 1927, the British factory concentrated on trucks.

Of the other countries, Germany's slow and painful recovery was delayed by a ban on imports imposed by her former enemies, and even where no actual embargo attained she was prevented from displaying her wares at the Motor Shows—German cars did not reappear at Olympia until 1927. Though Belgium made a miraculous recovery from the German occupation, she was fighting the American assemblers at home, and the might of Britain and France in dwindling foreign markets. Minerva (61) could work annual production up to two thousand units in the middle 1920s, but the nation's over-reliance on British buyers told against the industry in the end. The same went for Austria, who had virtually no home market since the carving-up of the Habsburg Empire; not even the best that Ferdinand Porsche and Karl Rabe could devise was competitive any more. Holland's Spyker (62) and Switzerland's Martini (53) were just solid, well-made cars with no particular

cachet except their nationality, and no money left in the kitty to take on the big battalions. In any case, the best-selling *marque* in Switzerland was Agnelli's FIAT from the other side of the Alps, and by 1923 FIAT disposed of a big luxury model, the 519, even if this was not a particularly good car.

Elsewhere, the establishment of national industry was stifled by the Detroit octopus. By the end of our period Sweden had only one active manufacturer of passenger cars, Thulin, who made German Agas under licence: Scania-Vabis had abdicated into heavy trucks. There was likewise no future for Australian cars; patriots might feel it their duty to buy an Australian Six (39), but it was only a hodgepodge of American parts, and Chevrolets, Dodges, and Buicks offered the same performance for less money, not to mention an integrated spares service. Empire-minded Canadians could also comfort themselves with the fact that the Buick they bought was (technically) a McLaughlin Buick made by fellow citizens of King George V in Oshawa, Ontario.

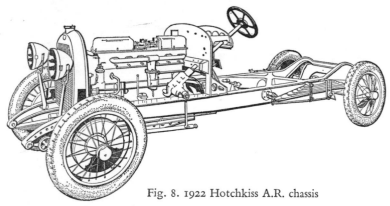

Fig. 8. 1922 Hotchkiss A.R. chassis

AUTHOR'S NOTES

The dates given to the cars painted are usually of the particular vehicles illustrated, or, if the precise date is unknown, of the currency of the model. A reference to the descriptive text under 'Passenger Cars in Detail' (pp. 97–153) will tell the reader which applies.

The colouring of a car as shown is not necessarily that in which it was normally seen or catalogued. It has been dictated by the exigencies of an attractive page layout. In many instances, though, cars were to be seen, if not catalogued, in almost any colour, since this could be at the discretion of the buyer (particularly in the cases of custom-built bodies).

For the sake of interest and to provide an idea of the variety to be seen on the basic model, different body styles, etc., are illustrated, even if unusual, i.e. they are not necessarily representative. Any two views of one car are not necessarily to scale; nor are the views of different cars on the same or adjoining pages.

Approximate conversion of cylinder bore and stroke: 25·4 millimetres (mm.) = 1 inch.

Approximate conversion of engine cubic capacity: 16·4 cubic centimetres (c.c.) = 1 cubic inch.

1

Hudson 37. 1913. U.S.A. Water-cooled, four vertical cylinders in line. 101·6×133·4 mm., 4352 cc. Side valves. Coil ignition. Three forward speeds. Shaft and bevel drive. Front, half-elliptic springs, rear three-quarter elliptic springs.

2

Saxon Model-A. 1913 (bottom). Model-14. 1916 (top). U.S.A. Water-cooled, four vertical cylinders in line. (bottom) 67×102 mm., 1430 cc.; (top) 69×102 mm., 1526 cc. Side valves. Coil ignition. (bottom) Two forward speeds. (top) Three forward speeds. Shaft and bevel drive. Quarter-elliptic springs front and rear.

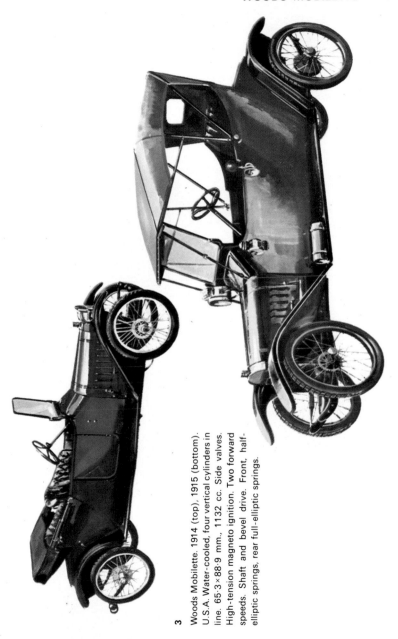

3

Woods Mobilette. 1914 (top). 1915 (bottom). U.S.A. Water-cooled, four vertical cylinders in line. 65·3 × 88·9 mm., 1132 cc. Side valves. High-tension magneto ignition. Two forward speeds. Shaft and bevel drive. Front, half-elliptic springs, rear full-elliptic springs.

LA BUIRE

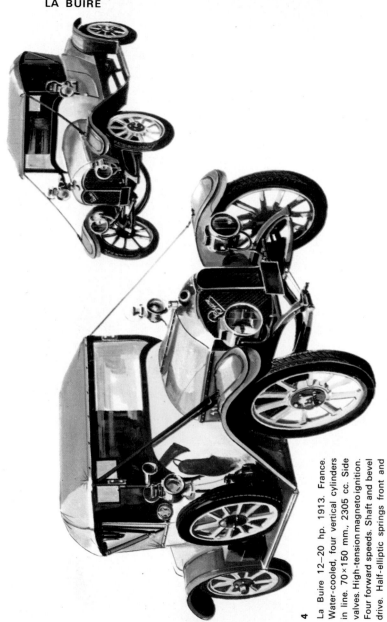

4

La Buire 12–20 hp. 1913. France. Water-cooled, four vertical cylinders in line. 70×150 mm., 2305 cc. Side valves. High-tension magneto ignition. Four forward speeds. Shaft and bevel drive. Half-elliptic springs front and rear.

5

Peugeot 'Bebe'. 1913. France. Water-cooled, four vertical cylinders in line. 55×90 mm., 856 cc. Side valves in T-head. High-tension magneto ignition. Two forward speeds. Front, half-elliptic springs, rear reversed quarter-elliptic springs.

VERMOREL

6

Vermorel 12CV. 1913. France. Water-cooled, four vertical cylinders in line. 74×120 mm., 2064 cc. Side valves. High-tension magneto ignition. Four forward speeds. Shaft drive. Front, half-elliptic springs, rear three-quarter elliptic springs.

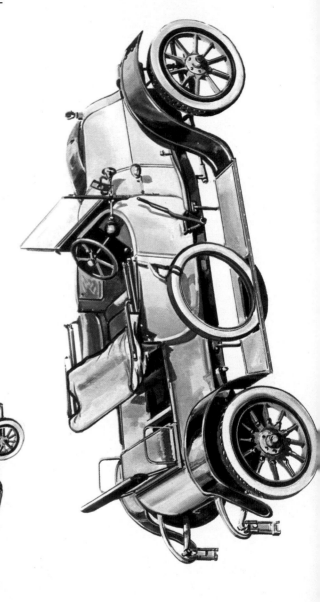

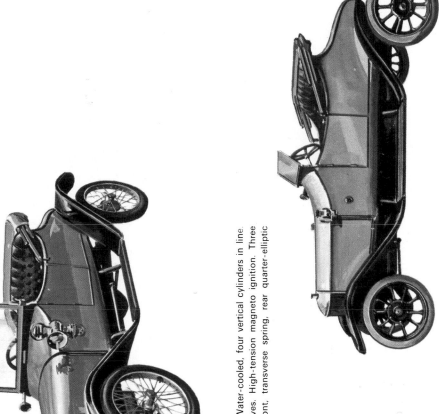

A.C.

7

A.C. 10 hp. 1913. Great Britain. Water-cooled, four vertical cylinders in line. 59×100 mm., 1094 cc. Side valves. High-tension magneto ignition. Three forward speeds. Worm drive. Front, transverse spring, rear quarter-elliptic springs.

8

Argyll 15—30 hp., 1913 (top), 15·9 hp., 1920 (bottom). Great Britain. Water-cooled, four vertical cylinders in line. 80×130 mm., 2614 cc. Single sleeve valves. High-tension magneto ignition. Four forward speeds. (Top) Shaft and worm drive, (bottom) spiral bevel drive. (Top) Front, half-elliptic springs, rear three-quarter elliptic springs; (bottom) front half-elliptic springs, rear cantilever springs.

9

Calcott 10·5 hp. 1913. Great Britain. Water-cooled, four vertical cylinders in line. 65×110 mm., 1460 cc. Side valves. High-tension magneto ignition. Three forward speeds. Shaft and bevel drive. Half-elliptic springs front and rear.

HUMBERETTE

10

Humberette. 1913. Great Britain. Air-cooled, two cylinders in vee formation. 84×90 mm., 998 cc. Side valves. High-tension magneto ignition. Three forward speeds. Shaft and bevel drive. Front, transverse spring, rear quarter-elliptic springs.

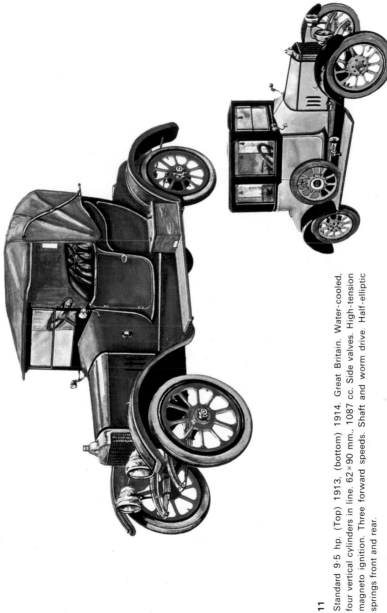

11

Standard 9·5 hp. (Top) 1913, (bottom) 1914. Great Britain. Water-cooled, four vertical cylinders in line. 62×90 mm., 1087 cc. Side valves. High-tension magneto ignition. Three forward speeds. Shaft and worm drive. Half-elliptic springs front and rear.

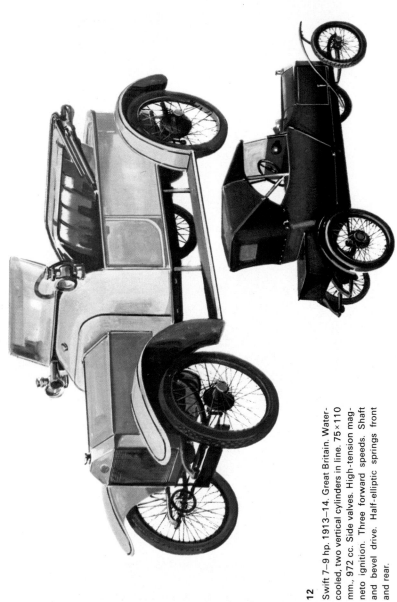

12

Swift 7–9 hp. 1913–14. Great Britain. Water-cooled, two vertical cylinders in line. 75×110 mm., 972 cc. Side valves. High-tension magneto ignition. Three forward speeds. Shaft and bevel drive. Half-elliptic springs front and rear.

13

Presto 10/30 PS. 1914 (top): 8/26 PS. 1913 (bottom). Germany. Water-cooled, four vertical cylinders in line. (Top) 80×130 mm., 2614 cc., (bottom) 75×120 mm., 2121 cc. Side valves. High-tension magneto ignition. Four forward speeds. Shaft and bevel drive. Half-elliptic springs front and rear.

ZÜST

14

Züst 25/35 hp. 1913. Italy. Water-cooled, four vertical cylinders in line. 100×150 mm., 4714 cc. Side valves. High-tension magneto ignition. Shaft and bevel drive. Front, half-elliptic springs, rear half-elliptic and cantilever springs.

15

Graf *und* Stift 45PS. 1913. Austria. Water-cooled, four vertical cylinders in line. 125×150 mm., 7320 cc. Side valves. High-tension magneto ignition. Four forward speeds. Shaft drive with de Dion back axle. Half-elliptic springs front and rear.

16

Fischer 10/33 CV. 1913. Switzerland. Water-cooled, four vertical cylinders in line. 85×120 mm., 2720 cc. Single sleeve valves. High-tension magneto ignition. Four forward speeds. Shaft and bevel drive. Front, half-elliptic springs, rear full-elliptic springs.

17

Detroit Electric. (Top) 1914, (bottom) 1918. U.S.A. Single electric motor under floor. Lever steering. Five forward speeds. Front, half-elliptic springs, rear full-elliptic springs.

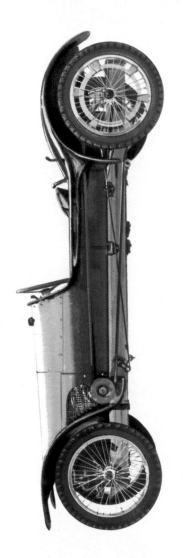

18

Imp Cyclecar. 1914. U.S.A. Air-cooled, two cylinders in vee formation. 85·7×95 mm., 1096 cc. Overhead valves. Coil ignition. Four forward speeds. Belt drive. Independent transverse springs front and rear.

19

Maxwell 50−6. 1914. U.S.A. Water-cooled, six vertical cylinders in line. 104·8×120·7 mm., 6246 cc. Side valves. High-tension magneto and coil ignition. Three forward speeds. Shaft and bevel drive. Front, half-elliptic springs, rear three-quarter elliptic springs.

TRUMBULL

20

Trumbull. 1914. U.S.A. Water-cooled, four vertical cylinders in line. 73×102 mm., 1708 cc. Side valves. High-tension magneto ignition. Three forward speeds. Bevel drive. Transverse springs front and rear.

21

G.W.K. 1914. Great Britain. Water-cooled, two vertical cylinders in line. 86×92 mm., 1069 cc. Side valves. High-tension magneto ignition. Four forward speeds. Bevel drive. Half-elliptic springs front and rear.

22

Mendip 11 hp. 1914. Great Britain. Water-cooled, four vertical cylinders in line. 67 × 90 mm., 1255 cc. Side valves in T-head. High-tension magneto ignition. Three forward speeds. Shaft and worm drive. Half-elliptic springs front and rear.

23

Adier 5/13 P S Modell-K. 1914. Germany. Water-cooled, four vertical cylinders in line. 65×98 mm., 1292 cc. Side valves. High-tension magneto ignition. Three forward speeds. Shaft drive. Half-elliptic springs front and rear.

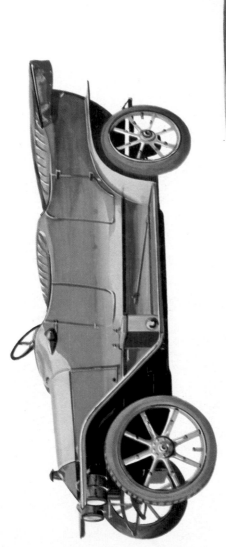

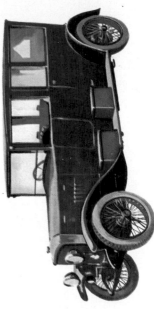

24

Bergmann-Metallurgique 10/30PS. 1914 (top), 1922 (bottom). Germany. Water-cooled, four vertical cylinders in line. 80×130 mm., 2614 cc. Side valves. High-tension magneto ignition. Four forward speeds. Shaft drive. Half-elliptic springs front and rear.

25

Dixi R.12 10/26 PS. 1914. Germany. Water-cooled, four vertical cylinders in line. 87×110 mm., 2598 cc. Side valves. High-tension magneto ignition. Four forward speeds. Shaft and bevel drive. Front, half-elliptic springs, rear three-quarter elliptic springs.

WANDERER

26

Wanderer (top) 5/12 PS, 1914, (bottom) 5/15 PS, 1918. Germany. Water-cooled four vertical cylinders in line. (Top) 62×95 mm., 1145 cc., (bottom) 64·5×100 mm., 1220 cc. (Top) Overhead inlet and side exhaust valves, (bottom) overhead valves. High-tension magneto ignition. Three forward speeds. Shaft and bevel drive. Front, half-elliptic springs, rear three-quarter elliptic springs.

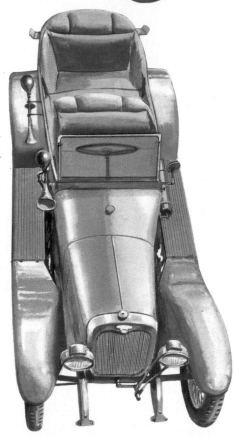

27

Isotta Fraschini OC5. 1914/15. Italy. Water-cooled, four vertical cylinders in
line. 100×140 mm., 4398 cc. Side valves. High-tension magneto ignition.
Shaft and bevel drive. Front, half-elliptic springs, rear three-quarter elliptic
springs.

LANCIA

28

Lancia 'Theta'. 1914. Italy. Water-cooled. four vertical cylinders in line. 110×130 mm., 4942 cc. Side valves. High-tension magneto ignition. Four forward speeds. Shaft and bevel drive. Half-elliptic springs front and rear.

29

F.N. 1250. 1914. Belgium. Water-cooled, four vertical cylinders in line. 60×110 mm., 1244 cc. Side valves. High-tension magneto ignition. Three forward speeds. Shaft and bevel drive. Front, half-elliptic springs, rear double half-elliptic springs.

30

Scania-Vabis. 1914. Sweden. Water-cooled, four vertical cylinders in line. 78×110 mm., 2102 cc. Side valves. High-tension magneto ignition. Four forward speeds. Shaft and bevel drive. Front, half-elliptic springs, rear three-quarter elliptic springs.

31

Russell-Knight 28. 1914. Canada. Water-cooled, four vertical cylinders in line. Double sleeve valves. High-tension magneto ignition. Three forward speeds. Shaft and bevel drive. Front, half-elliptic springs, rear three-quarter elliptic springs.

BREWSTER

32

Brewster. 1915 (top), 1919 (bottom). U.S.A. Water-cooled, four vertical cylinders in line. 101·6×139·7 mm., 4536 cc. Double sleeve valves. High-tension magneto ignition. Three forward speeds. Spiral bevel drive. Front, half-elliptic springs, rear cantilever springs.

33

Dodge Brothers' Four. 1915. U.S.A. Water-cooled, four vertical cylinders in line. 98·4×114·3 mm., 3478 cc. Side valves. Coil ignition. Three forward speeds. Front, half-elliptic springs, rear three-quarter elliptic springs.

PIERCE-ARROW

34

Pierce-Arrow 48. 1915. U.S.A. Water-cooled, six vertical cylinders in line. 114·3×139·7 mm., 8577 cc. Side valves in T-head. High tension magneto and coil ignition. Four forward speeds. Shaft and bevel drive. Front, half-elliptic springs, rear three-quarter elliptic springs.

35

Packard Twin-Six. 1916 (top), 1921 (bottom). U.S.A. Water-cooled, twelve cylinders in vee formation. 76·2×127 mm., 6950 cc. Side valves. Coil ignition. Three forward speeds. Spiral bevel drive. Half-elliptic springs front and rear.

36

Morris-Cowley. 1916. Great Britain. Water-cooled, four vertical cylinders in line. 69 × 100 mm., 1496 cc. Side valves. High-tension magneto ignition. Three forward speeds. Spiral bevel drive. Front, half-elliptic springs, rear three-quarter elliptic springs.

37

Buick Six. 1918. U.S.A. Water-cooled, six vertical cylinders in line. 85·7×114·3 mm., 3957 cc. Overhead valves. Coil ignition. Three forward speeds. Spiral bevel drive. Front, half-elliptic springs, rear cantilever springs.

38

Bjering. 1918—20. Norway. Air-cooled, four cylinders in vee formation. 79×108 mm., 2117 cc. Overhead valves. Magneto ignition. Three forward speeds. Shaft drive. Front, transverse spring, rear double transverse springs.

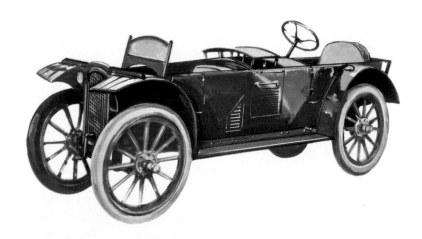

39

Australian Six. 1918 (top), 1920 (bottom). Australia. Water-cooled, six vertical cylinders in line. 79·4×127 mm., 3773 cc. Coil ignition. Three forward speeds. Spiral bevel drive. Half-elliptic springs front and rear.

Mathis SB. 1919, 1923. France. Water-cooled, four vertical cylinders in line. 60×100 mm., 1131 cc. Side valves. High-tension magneto ignition. Four forward speeds. Shaft and bevel drive. Half-elliptic springs front and rear.

41

Crossley 25–30 hp. 1919. Great Britain. Water-cooled, four vertical cylinders in line. 101·6×139·7 mm., 4536 cc. Side valves. High-tension magneto ignition. Four forward speeds. Spiral bevel drive. Half-elliptic springs front and rear.

LANCHESTER

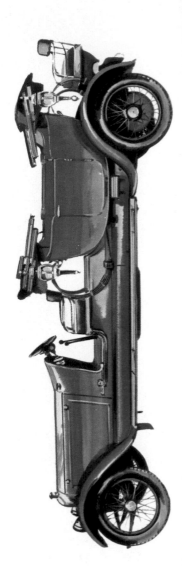

42

Lanchester 40. 1919. Great Britain. Water-cooled, six vertical cylinders in line. 101·6×127 mm., 6178 cc. Overhead camshaft. High-tension magneto coil ignition. Three forward speeds. Shaft and worm drive. Front, half-elliptic springs, rear cantilever springs.

PICCARD

43

Piccard-Pictet 15CV. 1919. Switzerland. Water-cooled, four vertical cylinders in line. 85×130 mm., 2950 cc. Single sleeve valves. High-tension magneto ignition. Four forward speeds. Shaft and bevel drive. Half-elliptic springs front and rear.

APPERSON

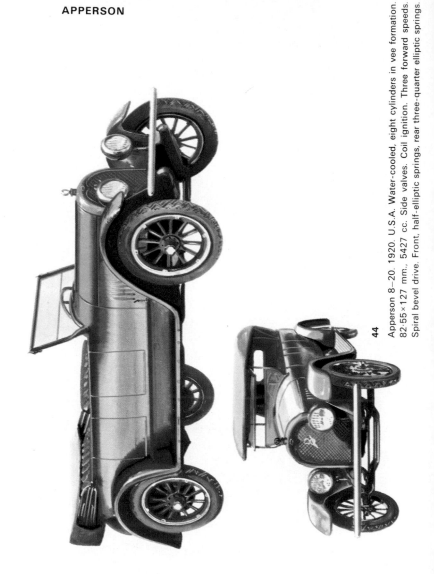

Apperson 8–20. 1920. U.S.A. Water-cooled, eight cylinders in vee formation. 82·55 × 127 mm., 5427 cc. Side valves. Coil ignition. Three forward speeds. Spiral bevel drive. Front, half-elliptic springs, rear three-quarter elliptic springs.

45

Briggs and Stratton Flyer. 1920. U.S.A. Air-cooled, single vertical cylinder. 63·5×63·5 mm., 201 cc. Side valves. Flywheel magneto ignition. No gears. Fifth wheel drive. No suspension.

ESSEX

46

Essex Four. 1920 (bottom), 1921 (top). U.S.A. Water-cooled, four vertical cylinders in line. 85·7×127 mm., 2924 cc. Overhead inlet and side exhaust valves. Coil ignition. Three forward speeds. Spiral bevel drive. Half-elliptic springs front and rear.

47

Ford Model-T. 1920. U.S.A. Water-cooled, four vertical cylinders in line. 95·2×101·6 mm., 2898 cc. Side valves. Flywheel magneto and trembler coil ignition. Two forward speeds. Shaft and bevel drive. Transverse springs front and rear.

Darracq Type-A 25CV. 1920. France. Water-cooled, eight cylinders in vee formation. 75×130 mm., 4594 cc. Side valves. Coil ignition. Four forward speeds. Spiral bevel drive. Front, half-elliptic springs, rear cantilever springs.

49

Carden 7–8 hp. 1920. Great Britain. Air-cooled, two horizontal cylinders side by side. 75×80 mm., 707 cc. Two-stroke. High-tension magneto ignition. Two forward speeds. Direct drive to back axle. Coil springs front and rear.

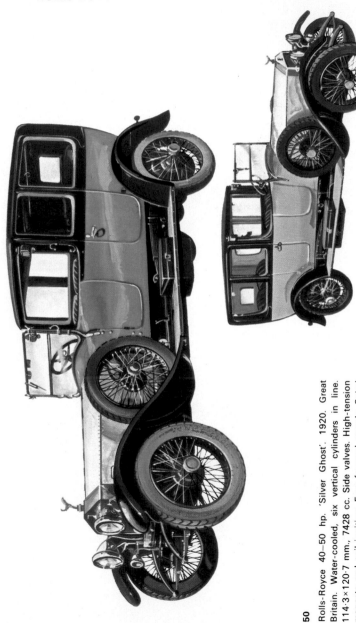

50

Rolls-Royce 40–50 hp. 'Silver Ghost'. 1920. Great Britain. Water-cooled, six vertical cylinders in line. 114·3×120·7 mm., 7428 cc. Side valves. High-tension magneto and coil ignition. Four forward speeds. Spiral bevel drive. Front, half-elliptic springs, rear cantilever springs.

51

Aga 4/20 PS. 1920. Germany. Water-cooled, four vertical cylinders in line.
64×110 mm., 1410 cc. Side valves. High-tension magneto ignition. Three
forward speeds. Shaft and bevel drive. Half-elliptic springs front and rear.

ANSALDO

52

Ansaldo 4C. 1920. Italy. Water-cooled, four vertical cylinders in line. 70×120 mm., 1847 cc. Overhead camshaft. High-tension magneto ignition. Three forward speeds. Spiral bevel drive. Half-elliptic springs front and rear.

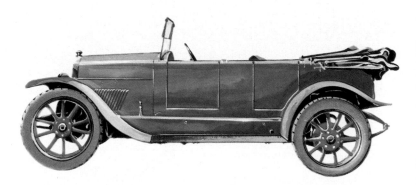

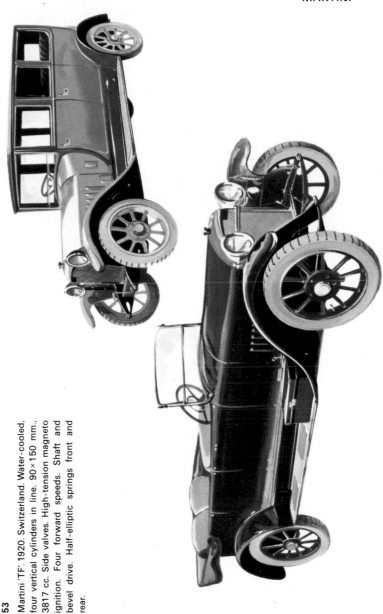

Martini 'TF'. 1920. Switzerland. Water-cooled, four vertical cylinders in line. 90×150 mm., 3817 cc. Side valves. High-tension magneto ignition. Four forward speeds. Shaft and bevel drive. Half-elliptic springs front and rear.

BERLIET

54

Berliet 'VL' 16CV. 1921. France. Water-cooled, four vertical cylinders in line. 90×130 mm., 3308 cc. Side valves. High-tension magneto ignition. Three forward speeds. Spiral bevel drive. Front, half-elliptic springs, rear cantilever springs.

55

De Dion-Bouton 10CV. 1921. France. Water-cooled, four vertical cylinders in line. 70×120 mm., 1847 cc. Side valves. High-tension magneto ignition. Four forward speeds. Shaft and bevel drive. Front, half-elliptic springs, rear cantilever springs.

56

Voisin C4. 1921, 1923. France. Water-cooled, four vertical cylinders in line. 60×110 mm., 1244 cc. Double sleeve valves. High-tension magneto ignition. Four forward speeds. Spiral bevel drive. Half-elliptic springs front and rear.

57

Leyland Eight. 1921 (bottom), 1923 (top). Great Britain. Water-cooled eight vertical cylinders in line. 89×146 mm., 7266 cc. Overhead camshaft. Coil ignition. Four forward speeds. Spiral bevel drive. Front, half-elliptic springs, rear quarter-elliptic springs and torsion bar.

STAR

58

Star 11·9 hp. 1921/22. Great Britain. Water-cooled, four vertical cylinders in line. 69×120 mm., 1795 cc. Side valves. High-tension magneto ignition. Three forward speeds. Spiral bevel drive. Half-elliptic springs front and rear.

59

Rumpler OA. 104. 1921. Germany. Water-cooled, six cylinders in W-formation. 74×100 mm., 2581 cc. Overhead valves. High-tension magneto ignition. Three forward speeds. Spiral bevel drive. Front, half-elliptic springs, rear independent swing axles.

Moto-Cor. 1921. Italy. Air-cooled, two horizontally-opposed cylinders. 78×78 mm., 745 cc. Overhead valves. High-tension magneto ignition. Three forward speeds. Chain drive. Half-elliptic springs front and rear.

61

Minerva 30CV. 1921. Belgium. Water-cooled, six vertical cylinders in line. 90×140 mm., 5344 cc. Double sleeve valves. High-tension magneto ignition. Four forward speeds. Spiral bevel drive. Front, half-elliptic springs, rear cantilever springs.

62

Spyker 30/40 hp. 1921. The Netherlands. Water-cooled, six vertical cylinders in line. 95×135 mm., 5741 cc. Side valves. High-tension magneto ignition. Four forward speeds. Spiral bevel drive. Half-elliptic springs front and rear.

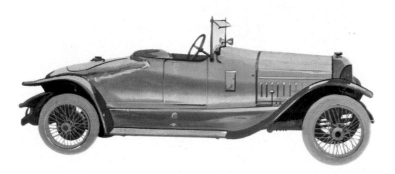

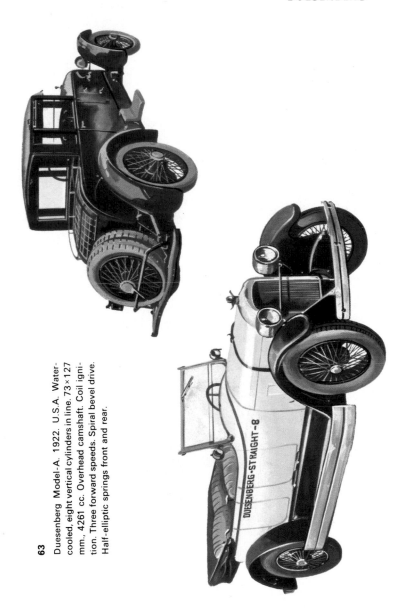

63

Duesenberg Model-A. 1922. U.S.A. Water-cooled, eight vertical cylinders in line. 73×127 mm., 4261 cc. Overhead camshaft. Coil ignition. Three forward speeds. Spiral bevel drive. Half-elliptic springs front and rear.

TEMPLAR

64

Templar. 1922. U.S.A. Water-cooled, four vertical cylinders in line. 85·7×139·7 mm., 3227 cc. Overhead valves. High-tension magneto ignition. Three forward speeds. Spiral bevel drive. Half-elliptic springs front and rear.

65

Wills Sainte Claire. 1922. U.S.A. Water-cooled, eight cylinders in vee formation. 82·55×101·6 mm., 4350 cc. Overhead camshaft. Coil ignition. Three forward speeds. Spiral bevel drive. Half-elliptic springs front and rear.

CYCLAUTO

66

Cyclauto. 1922. France. Water-cooled, four vertical cylinders in line. 55×100 mm., 950 cc. Overhead camshaft. High-tension magneto ignition. Three forward speeds. Shaft and bevel drive. Double quarter-elliptic springs front and rear.

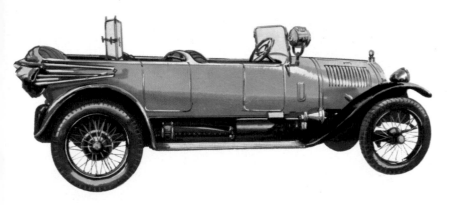

67

Hotchkiss 'AL'. 1922. France. Water-cooled, four vertical cylinders in line. 95×140 mm., 3969 cc. Overhead valves. High-tension magneto ignition. Four forward speeds. Spiral bevel drive. Front, half-elliptic springs, rear cantilever springs.

RENAULT

68

Renault 6CV. 1922 (top), 1923 (bottom). France. Water-cooled, four vertical cylinders in line. 58×90 mm., 951 cc. Side valves. High-tension magneto ignition. Three forward speeds. Spiral bevel drive. Front, half-elliptic springs, rear transverse spring.

STONELEIGH

69

Stoneleigh 9 hp. 1922. Great Britain. Air-cooled, two cylinders in vee formation. 85×88 mm., 998 cc. Overhead valves. Coil ignition. Three forward speeds. Spiral bevel drive. Quarter-elliptic springs front and rear.

O.M.

70

O.M. *Tipo* 469. 1922. Italy. Water-cooled, four vertical cylinders in line. 69×100 mm., 1496 cc. Side valves. Coil ignition. Shaft and bevel drive. Half-elliptic springs front and rear.

71

Dobie E-13. 1923. U.S.A. Steam engine, double-acting cross-compound four horizontal cylinders. Bore (high-pressure cylinders) 68 mm., (low pressure cylinders) 114·3 mm. Stroke 127 mm. Monotube vertical boiler. Electrical ignition. Direct drive to back axle. Half-elliptic springs front and rear.

72

Nash Four. 1922, 1923. U.S.A. Water-cooled, four vertical cylinders in line. 85·7×127 mm., 2924 cc. Overhead valves. Coil ignition. Three forward speeds. Spiral bevel drive. Half-elliptic springs front and rear.

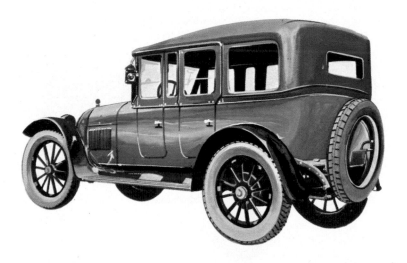

73

Citroen 5CV. 1923. France. Water-cooled, four vertical cylinders in line. 55 × 90 mm., 856 cc. Side valves. High-tension magneto ignition. Three forward speeds. Spiral bevel drive. Quarter-elliptic springs front and rear.

74

Leyat. 1923. France. Air-cooled, two cylinders, horizontally-opposed. 91·5 × 91·5 mm., 1198 cc. Overhead valves. High-tension magneto ignition. No gears. Tractor airscrew drive. Front, cantilever springs, rear coil springs.
(*For other details, see text*)

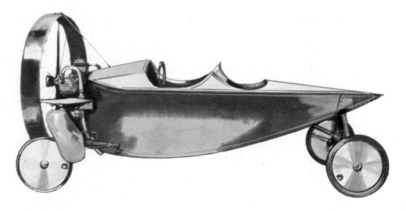

75

Zedel 11CV. 1923. France. Water-cooled, four vertical cylinders in line. 75×120 mm., 2121 cc. Side valves. High-tension magneto ignition. Four forward speeds. Helical bevel drive. Half-elliptic springs front and rear.

NAPIER

76

Napier 40–50 hp. 1923. Great Britain. Water-cooled, six vertical cylinders in line. 101·6×127 mm., 6178 cc. Overhead camshaft. High-tension magneto and coil ignition. Four forward speeds. Spiral bevel drive. Front, half-elliptic springs, rear cantilever springs.

77

Trojan 'PB'. Great Britain. Water-cooled, four cylinders in 'square' formation, horizontally disposed. 63·5×120·7 mm., 1523 cc. Two-stroke. Coil ignition. Two forward speeds. Central chain drive. Cantilever springs front and rear.

78

Audi 'K' 14/50 PS. 1923. Germany. Water-cooled, four vertical cylinders in line. 90×140 mm., 3563 cc. Overhead valves. High-tension magneto ignition. Four forward speeds. Spiral bevel drive. Half-elliptic springs front and rear.

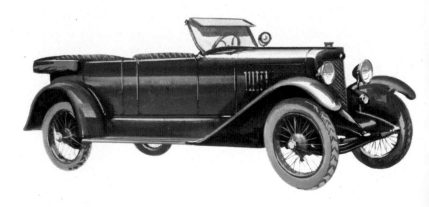

FIAT

79

Fiat *Tipo* 501. 1923. Italy. Water-cooled, four vertical cylinders in line. 65×110 mm., 1460 cc. Side valves. High-tension magneto ignition. Four forward speeds. Spiral bevel drive. Half-elliptic springs front and rear.

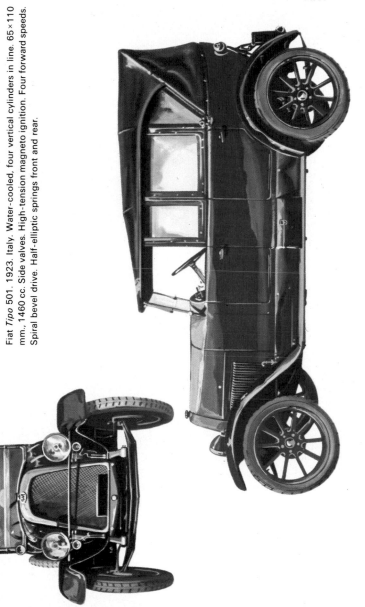

80

Lila. 1923. Japan. Air-cooled, four vertical cylinders in line. Shaft drive. No further details available.

PASSENGER CARS IN DETAIL

1 HUDSON 37, 1913, U.S.A.

Financed by J. L. Hudson, the Detroit department-store magnate, Hudson was one of the younger American makes, first seen in July 1909 as a straightforward 20 h.p. four-cylinder retailing at a round thousand dollars. 1910 sales of 4,556 units were promising, and in 1913 deliveries were up to 6,401, sufficient to make the Hudson America's tenth best seller.

Model-37 was the last four to bear the name, and in many ways typifies the middle-class American automobile of its period. The side-valve monobloc engine is splash-lubricated (as were all Hudsons up to 1942), and three forward speeds are the norm: a typical feature is Hudson's wet-plate clutch, which also survived until Pearl Harbour days. For a price in the region of $1,600 (£325) a buyer was entitled to expect electric lights and a starter, and attempts are already being made to introduce an element of streamline into the body, the sidelamps being faired into the firewall as on contemporary Peerlesses and Ramblers. Closed bodywork was, however, still in its infancy, and in coupé guise the 37 resembles a sentry-box on wheels, even if Hudson avoided the 'colonial' extravaganzas affected by Haynes and others.

The 37 was quite a brisk performer, and the range of fours included a Mercer-style raceabout with bolster tank publicised as the 'Mile-A-Minute' model. In 1914 A. Rawlinson, the English importer, chose the now obsolete four for his Tourist Trophy entry, though this was unfortunately a non-starter due to mechanical troubles in practice.

Hudson's future, of course, lay with the six-cylinder engine, and already in 1913 they were offering the big 6–54, a 3,000-pounder on a 127-inch wheelbase which sold for $2,350 (£470). A smaller 6–40 followed in 1915, and a year later came the first of the legendary Super Sixes, renowned both for their exploits on America's speedways and as the mainstay of New Zealand's service-car network.

2 SAXON MODEL-A, 1913, MODEL-14, 1916, U.S.A.

Several manufacturers tried to woo the American motorist away from big cars with lightly-stressed engines, and of these early compacts the Saxon was perhaps the most successful. Introduced in 1913, it sold 19,000 in its third season, and a year later, in 1916, no fewer than 27,800 were delivered, putting the *marque* in eighth place in national sales.

The recipe was simple: scale down the established American theme and keep it a two-seater. In its original form the car used a four-cylinder Continental engine (though Ferro units were also fitted) similar to that found in the first Morris-Cowleys; a two-speed sliding-type gearbox was mounted in unit with the back axle. For a modest $395 (about £80) buyers got a windshield, acetylene lamps, and tools, though the first Saxons lacked dashboards and rode on spidery wire wheels—after 1914 most customers specified the optional wood artilleries. Top speed was round

40 m.p.h., and a fuel consumption of 35 m.p.g. meant petrol bills at the rate of only half a cent per mile.

The Saxon outsold and outlived cyclecars like the Imp and the Woods-Mobilette. The Model-14 of 1916 had three forward speeds though it retained the old transaxle, and an enlarged engine disposed of 18 b.h.p. Electric lighting and starting were still extras; the fours were continued into 1917 with little or no change. Alas, Saxon made an all-too-common mistake, essaying the cheap family-car market with a 2·9-litre six-cylinder, the S2, on a 112-inch wheelbase at $785. Here they were competing against Dodge, Overland, and the smaller Studebakers.

In 1918 thirty-eight Saxon Sixes raced in relays from New York to San Francisco, setting up a record aggregate trans-Continental time of 6 days 18 hours 10 minutes, but three years later the company tried another four, the family-sized Saxon-Duplex. This was no bargain at $1,675, and sales were negligible. After 1922 the make was no longer quoted.

3 WOODS-MOBILETTE,
1914, 1915, U.S.A.

The cyclecar craze hit the United States in 1913, and well over a hundred manufacturers tried their hand at the game. Inevitably, many resorted to motorcycle engines and belt drive, but Francis Woods's contribution was more substantially built, as well as surviving until 1917 and enjoying a minor vogue.

The designer's objective was compactness, and Woods claimed that his Mobilette could be stored 'beside the icebox or the kitchen table'. While this was questionable, the air-cooled tandem-seater prototype of 1910 was a mere 35 inches wide, in spite of which it ran to four vertical cylinders (concealed beneath a Renault or Franklin-style hood), a channel steel frame, bevel drive, and a differential back axle. The transmission was of two-speed planetary type, and the front track was thirty inches. Intensive testing led to greater sophistication, and the Woods offered to the public at $380 (£76) had a water-cooled engine, two forward speeds selected by an orthodox central lever, and all its brakes on the rear wheels. Tandem seating was retained for the neat body, while on an advertised 12 b.h.p. the car attained a rather laboured 35 m.p.h. The leather cone clutch, it would seem, was either 'in' or 'out', and the steering was extremely high-geared.

Initially cars were assembled in a small loft in South Michigan Avenue, Chicago, but in August 1914 Woods moved to Harvey, Illinois, and series production got under way. Extras included a top and windshield ($15) and also offered were acetylene instead of the standard oil lamps, and a detachable back to transform the vehicle into a light delivery van. 1915 Mobilettes had the more sociable staggered seating, a more powerful engine, a lengthened wheelbase, and three-quarter elliptics at the rear, while the last cars boasted three forward speeds, and weather protection was now inclusive at the unaltered price of $380. Output was now said to be 22 b.h.p., but most of the cars sold in 1917 were marketed as light commercials under the name of Sheridan.

4 LA BUIRE 12–20 h.p., 1913, France

Lyons ranked second to Paris as a car-making centre, and the Chantiers de la Buire were one of the principal manufacturers. Starting with sub-contract work on Léon Serpollet's steamers in 1900, they progressed to complete petrol cars in 1904; these were conventional chain-driven affairs with T headed engines, though some had Rover-type compression brakes. A characteristic of *Lyonnais* industry—and this applied to Berliet and Rochet-Schneider—was a lack of interest in racing (though a La Buire finished second in the 1907 Coupe de la Commission Sportive). Instead they preferred to concentrate on sprints and hill-climbs; Joseph Higginson's enormous 80 h.p. La Buire was almost unbeatable in England in the 1907–12 period, and can claim to have inspired the original 30–98 Vauxhall, since this was conceived by its owner as a replacement for the ageing monster.

The company was hard hit by the Agadir Crisis of 1907, and for a short while in 1909–10 the cars were put out as Berthiers until more capital was forthcoming and an even tenor was resumed. Though an elephantine 9½-litre six was still offered in 1910, La Buire were moving towards the accepted European idiom—side-valve monobloc engines, high-tension magneto ignition, unit gearboxes and bevel drive. Multi-plate clutches were used, and the firm was among the first to adopt chain-driven camshafts. Unusual features were a rear axle with twin crown wheels and (on bigger versions) twin pedal-operated brakes, the second pedal being linked with the lever, and actuating drums on the rear wheels. Mechanical starters made their appearance in 1914, together with the fashionable vee-radiator, though La Buire's pre-1914 version was gently rounded.

Immensely long piston strokes were also a characteristic of the cars, their smallest 1913 model, the 10CV, having dimensions of 65×130 mm. This theme was pursued after the War with an electrically-equipped 75×150 mm. 12CV, wearing a taller radiator in the Panhard or Delahaye idiom. Four-wheel brakes came early (in 1922) and overhead valves a year later, but like many a French factory La Buire had nothing new to say after the Armistice. They died of atrophy in 1930.

5 PEUGEOT 'BEBE', 1913, France

Peugeot had already scored one light-car hit with their original 'Baby' (Type 37) of 1902, and by 1912 they were capable of true volume-production, to the tune of 3,000 cars in a year.

Built in the former Lion-Peugeot works at Beaulieu-Valentigney, the 'Bébé' was the work of Ettore Bugatti, and was probably his Type 12, though Peugeot called it the BP1. It was the smallest four-cylinder car on the market at the time of its introduction. Despite the archaic T-head layout, the 856 c.c. engine's output of 10 b.h.p. at 2,000 r.p.m. was sufficient to propel a two-seater weighing 730 pounds at 35 m.p.h. As on Bugatti's own cars, the simple chassis wore reversed quarter-elliptic springs at the rear, but though *le patron's* intention was to offer four or five forward speeds, the production version had only two. The ingenious transmission incorporated two concentric propeller shafts each driving bevels on the back axle, and ratios were selected by a sliding dog-clutch on the forward end of the shaft; there was a separate lever for reverse, which also coped with first gear on 1914 'Bébés'. These had three forward speeds, an arrangement necessitating a small gearbox at the front of the torque tube. Ratios were wide, but the car could cope with elegant little coupé bodies at the price of a reduced performance. It was respectable value at £160 in London, reduced to £125 by the beginning of 1915, when the standard coachwork was a sporty two-seater with bolster tank and flimsy cycle-type mudguards.

The drip-feed lubrication gave no trouble, and Bugatti's suspension was said to be light on tyres, which needed replacement only at 6,000-mile intervals—the price of a complete set was said to be a mere £5! However, owners who expected Bugatti-like precision of handling soon discovered that the Peugeot's directional stability was nil. When production was discontinued in 1916, 3,095 'Bébés' had been made, but the model was not revived after the War. Instead, the company made a fresh start with the narrow, tandem-seated Quadrilette (Type 161).

6 **VERMOREL 12CV**, 1913, France

The Vermorel was typical of many a smaller French *marque*. It was made at Villefranche-sur-Saône by a firm of general engineers and woodworkers who had been in the business since 1850, and had built prototype cars in 1897 and 1900. However M. Vermorel and his chief engineer Givaudan seem to have been more interested in aeronautics and aviation, and few if any Vermorels reached the general public before 1908. For the next twenty-two years automobiles were produced in modest numbers, though the company made most of the vehicle themselves, and were said to be employing 800 hands in 1911.

Early Vermorels had straightforward T-head four-cylinder engines, four forward speeds, shaft drive, and three-quarter elliptic rear suspension. Lubrication was by pressure and splash, and cooling by thermo-syphon. The long-stroke 12CV was an average performer (40–45 m.p.h.) and averagely priced (about £350 in England), but it was renowned for its top-gear flexibility, and an example tried by *The Motor* in 1911 proved capable of negotiating London traffic without a downward change. Though these cars were still offered in 1913, Vermorel were falling into line with contemporary practice, adopting the L-head configuration and block-cast cylinders on a new four, the 1,505 c.c. Type N. At the top of the immediate pre-War range was a 2·8-litre *Type Sport* with vee-radiator said to be capable of 72 m.p.h. Also in 1914 the 12CV gave way to a 2·3-litre LO-type in the new idiom, and this formed the basis for post-War models, now with unit gearboxes and full electrics.

Unfortunately the age of Citroën and Mathis was no time for small regional manufacturers; though Vermorel lasted longer than most, and were still turning out 300-odd cars a year as late as 1926. Four-wheel brakes appeared on the X-type of 1923, and this developed into the overhead-valve Z of 1925. There was even a 2-litre o.h.v. six, the 10CV AH2, in 1928. Vermorel are still in business as general engineers.

7 A.C. 10 h.p., 1913, Great Britain

The initials A.C. stood for Auto-Carrier, but the 10 h.p. of 1913 represented the first break with the old three-wheeler image, though the parcelcar and its passenger-carrying derivative, the Sociable, were continued until World War I.

The hallmark of John Weller's four-wheeled A.C.s was a three-speed gearbox mounted in unit with the worm-driven back axle, and incorporating an ingenious if singularly ineffective disc brake. This could be seen gently rotating at the exposed rear end when the car was in motion. The simple chassis frame anticipated the modern 'perimeter' type, and power was provided by an 1,100 c.c. two-bearing four-cylinder Fivet engine imported from France. The A.C. was modestly priced at £175, and a top speed of 45 m.p.h. was claimed.

By 1914 other body styles were available—a dainty little coupé, and an aluminium-panelled staggered-seat sports with central gear and brake levers. On 1915 versions the rear springs were flattened to give a lower build, and the adoption of a more powerful 1,327 c.c. engine enabled the A.C. to cope with four-seater bodywork. Signi-

ficantly, a new cyclecar combining the outward appearances and rack-and-pinion steering of the Ten with the Sociable's single-cylinder power unit, pedal-controlled epicyclic gear, and chain drive was stillborn.

The first post-War A.C.s used the Fivet engine, but this was soon replaced by the 1½-litre British Anzani, and the cars sold well despite an inflated price— £560 by early 1920. More important, the 1919 London Show had seen the début of that hardy perennial, Weller's 2-litre wet-liner overhead-camshaft six, which powered every A.C. made between 1929 and 1955 and was still available as late as 1963. When the great S. F. Edge took over as Governing Director in 1921 there was inevitably a greater emphasis on the six-cylinder types, though the fours still had plenty of life left in them, the Anzani giving way in 1925 to a similar A.C. design made for them by Cubitts of Aylesbury. But the company had lost interest in utility motoring for good—if one excepts the curious little 'Petite' three-wheelers of the 1950s.

8 ARGYLL 15–30 h.p., 1913, 15·9 h.p., 1920, Great Britain

Argyll had been one of the great British names in early days, and under the dynamic Alex Govan (who died in 1907) production had been worked up to over a thousand cars a year. Govan's death was not, however, the only disaster, for Argyll sunk a quarter of a million pounds into a vast factory at Alexandria-by-Glasgow which was never fully utilised. The money ran out for the first time in 1908, and did so irrevocably in June, 1914, thanks to protracted litigation with the Knight patentees over the Burt-McCollum single-sleeve-valve engine, and an abortive aero-engine programme. In the meantime Henri Perrot and Alex Davidson had created some very interesting cars.

These featured an efficient four-wheel braking system designed by J. M. Rubury (who sold his rights to Perrot for £200 when Argyll folded!). Unlike the contemporary British efforts of Arrol-Johnston and Crossley, these were of coupled type, diagonally compensated, and actuated by pedal and lever alike. First seen on the s.v. 12 h.p. in 1911, they were standardised on the 15–30 h.p. and 25–50 h.p. single-sleeve-valve models of 1912–14.

These latter were a commercial failure, and undoubtedly represented an extravagance to be avoided by firms as shaky as Argyll, but their reliability was revealed by the exploits of a tuned and lightened 15–30 at Brooklands in 1913. Output of the 2·6 litre unit was boosted from 32 b.h.p. to 55 b.h.p. at 2,800 r.p.m., and the Argyll's average speed over fourteen hours was 76·73 m.p.h. Unlike its rival, the Knight, the Burt engine laid no smokescreens, and a gallon of lubricant lasted a thousand miles.

Alas, the 15–30 was expensive: £495 was a lot of money in 1914, even if this price included a two-piece windshield, a one-man top, five detachable wire wheels, and electric side and tail lamps—the headlights were extra.

After the 1914 liquidation, John Brimlow acquired the remains of the company, and resumed production in the original Bridgeton works. The post-War 15·9 boasted an electric starter, a detachable head, and spiral bevel final drive, but it had rear-wheel brakes only. Worse still, Argyll now had to buy their engines (still Burts) from Greenwood and Batley of Leeds. In 1924, after the inflationary period, it cost £725 ($3,650)—no competition for the Austin Twenty (£625) or even Sunbeam's 14–40 at £685. Only eleven 15·9s were sold in five seasons.

9 CALCOTT 10·5 h.p., 1913, Great Britain

Typical of the 1913 generation of big cars in miniature from British factories was the Calcott, product of a cycle firm founded in 1886. Since 1904 they had been building motorcycles, but abandoned this line of business when the cars started to prosper.

The Calcott was rather bigger than some of its contemporaries, with a capacity of nearly 1,500 c.c. Detachable artillery wheels were standard from the start, and the crankshaft boasted three main bearings. On a weight of 1,288 pounds it was capable of 45 m.p.h., and its makers claimed 40 m.p.g., though 30 was nearer the truth. The handsome shouldered radiator had a hint of Standard about it, and by 1915 Calcotts were available with Efandem electric lighting which raised the price to £201 (about $1,000). Some elegant bodies were fitted, Hollick and Pratt contributing a two-seater cabriolet, while Harrods' department store made a speciality of a sporty three-seater cloverleaf, and Charlesworth built a fixed-head coupé.

The designer was A. Alderson, who had been responsible for the successful Singer Ten of 1912; but fortunately he used a conventionally-located separate three-speed gearbox instead of the Singer's troublesome transaxle. Calcott were, however, victims of old-fashioned workshop practice inherited from cycle days. To the end they had no coachworks, and no proper machine-shop, tool-room, or foundry: cylinders were bored on a home-made borer. Many parts had to be bought out, the chassis frames coming from Glasgow, and bodies from Coventry firms such as Pass or Cross and Ellis. Thus workmanship was indifferent, and the product uncompetitive. A revised 10·5 with lengthened wheelbase was announced in 1919, but Calcott were doomed once Morris launched his price-war. Alderson was succeeded by L. J. Shorter from Humber, who evolved a four-speed 12–24 with detachable cylinder head for 1924; a year later this one had acquired four-wheel brakes. For 1926 the firm joined the light-six vogue with a 2,565 c.c. 16–50 at £495, but despite a 60 m.p.h. top speed this was Calcott's swan-song.

10 **HUMBERETTE,** 1914, Great Britain

Humber had been responsible for Britain's first successful cheap runabout, the single-cylinder Humberette, in 1903, and at £147 this had many admirers, even if one unkind critic stigmatised its two forward speeds as 'slow and very slow'. Their next bargain-basement item, the 8 h.p. of 1908, was a biggish twin of some technical sophistication to which the public did not take kindly, but they redressed the adverse balance with the second Humberette of 1913.

Power was provided by an air-cooled vee-twin engine of motorcycle type, and the Duocar prototype of 1911 was a true cyclecar, with two-speed, pedal-controlled epicyclic gear. The engine sat well back in the frame behind a dummy radiator, giving it a racy look, and on a weight of 448 pounds it proved capable of 35 m.p.h. Humber hoped to market it at the magic £100. It was, however, dropped in favour of a conventional light car with three speed sliding-type box, leather cone clutch, and bevel drive. At £120 it was quite good value, and on 11 b.h.p. it would see an honest 40 m.p.h. Faults were an awkward quadrant change and rather critical lubrication by Best and Lloyd motorcycle-type drip feed. For those in quest of more refinement, there was a water-cooled version at £135, identical in appearance except that its radiator was a real one.

Production was on a sizeable scale: in 1913 Humber's 2,000 hands were making 60–70 Humberettes a week as well as a range of bigger cars, and both variants were continued until the factory converted to war work. They did not, however, make the mistake of resuscitating their twin-cylinder design after the Armistice. Indeed, their next small car was the exact antithesis of the Humberette—the refined 8–18 of 1923 with i.o.e. four-cylinder engine, appalling brakes, and superbly-executed coachwork. This line of thinking lasted until 1930, when under Rootes management the emphasis shifted to six-cylinder sedans of ambassadorial proportions.

11 STANDARD 9·5 h.p., 1913, 1914, Great Britain

Humber had always had a foot in the small-car camp. By contrast Standard's reputation had been made with cheap sixes energetically promoted by Sir Charles Friswell, who had managed to sell a whole fleet of them as official transport for King George V's Delhi Durbar of 1911.

By 1912, however, the motoring public had been disillusioned by a surfeit of indifferent six-cylinder models and their elephantine crankshaft 'periods'. Standard, therefore, made the wise decision to follow Singer into the small-car field, their contribution being unveiled in March, 1913, though none reached the customers for another five months. This 9·5 followed conventional practice, with s.v. monobloc engine and three-speed separate gearbox, though Standard were more conservative than Calcott in retaining a transmission footbrake, and overhead worm drive was preferred to the more familiar bevel. The 'Rhyl' two-seater body was very well equipped, and for the list price of £185 (hurriedly raised to £195 once deliveries started) one got a spare wheel with tyre, a top, a windshield, and five lamps, though a dickey seat was extra.

The Standard sold briskly abroad, and one example recorded a startling 50·7 m.p.g. in the R.A.C. of South Africa's Maitland–Caledon Trial. At home the *marque* collected a Gold Medal in the 1914 British Light Car Trials, and a class victory in that year's Irish event. A variety of body styles was offered, though Standard retained their 90-inch wheelbase and eschewed four-seaters. There were, however, a victoria, two types of light delivery van, and a closed coupé which cost £290 ($1,450) with Brolt electric lighting. From mid-1914 the radiators lost part of their shells, the tubes being exposed at the sides. When manufacture ceased 'for the duration' in 1915 production had been worked up to fifty 9·5s a week.

The model was briefly revived, with full electrics, in 1919, but better things were in store, and 1920 saw the first of a new generation of o.h.v. Standards, the 68 × 110 mm. SLO-type.

12 SWIFT 7–9 h.p., 1913, 1914, Great Britain

The old-established Swift concern, which had graduated to cars *via* sewing-machines, bicycles, and motor tricycles, followed the same course as Humber in their attack on the prosperous light-car market. What they termed a cyclecar was in fact a conventional automobile with a vertical-twin side-valve engine designed by W. Radford and made in their own factory.

As might be expected of an experienced builder of motorcycles, Swift experimented with air cooling on their 1912 prototype, but abandoned it in favour of water cooling with thermosyphon circulation. Car practice was also reflected in the chain-driven camshaft, leather cone clutch, three-speed box, gate change, and bevel-driven rear axle. Steering was by rack and pinion, and the tubular chassis was inswept at the front, with a separate sub-frame for engine and gearbox. The two seats were heavily staggered, not, as Swift pointed out, to reduce width, but to make it easier for the driver to get in and out. The first models wore a 'wedge' radiator which aped the then-fashionable Belgian Métallurgique (this make, be it said, and not the German Mercedes, was responsible for the vee-radiator mania of 1913–14), but in April, 1913, when more than 600 Swift cyclecars had been sold, a revised model appeared with a flat radiator, H-section front axle, and lengthened wheelbase. Acetylene lamps were standard equipment, but Joys of Coventry offered a sports two-seater with airship tail and electric lighting which was said to do 56 m.p.h.—an interesting thought on a mere 998 c.c.!

Just before War broke out, a new Radford design made its appearance—this was the four-cylinder Ten, the most successful of all the Swifts. It was made in various forms right up to the company's collapse in the early summer of 1931, but on the first 1915 models the leather cone clutch and semi-elliptic springs were identical with those on the cyclecar. Some leftover 7–9 h.p. Swift frames were also adapted to the Eric–Campbell light car of 1919.

13 PRESTO 8/26 PS, 1913, 10/30 PS, 1914, Germany

Imperial Germany supported a profusion of automobile manufacturers in 1914, though many of these were little known outside the German-speaking world; this despite the influence of events such as the Herkomer and Prince Henry Trials, which had accelerated engine development. Nor were all these cars enormous, for the 1914 Presto range embraced nothing larger than a 14/40 PS of 3,563 c.c.

The company's first serious attempt at car manufacture came in 1907, when they made French Delahayes under licence, before moving on to some 11-litre monsters which ran in the 1908 Prince Henry Trials, and to a 100 × 200 mm. four-cylinder in 1909. From 1910 onwards, however, they concentrated on orthodox medium-sized machinery of high quality which had only a limited sale; Presto lost money in 1911 and 1912.

Basic design features included L-head monobloc engines with enclosed valves, ball-bearing crankshafts, fuel feed by exhaust pressure, cone clutches, four-speed gearboxes and bevel drive, though lubrication was by the Friedmann splash system also used on contemporary Austro-Daimlers—full-pressure oiling did not arrive until 1914. Smallest Presto was the 1,544 6/18 PS introduced in 1913, and an ingenious feature of some 1914 models was an automatic switch which cut the ignition when oil pressure dropped to a dangerous level; a similar arrangement was found on sleeve-valve Panhards of the 1930s.

Like many parallel German firms, Presto had nothing new to offer after the Armistice, and until 1925 they were producing what was basically the old 1914 theme with full electrics—plus such refinements as detachable heads and four-wheel brakes. They joined the D.A.K. consortium in 1920, but though rationalisation was the object of such groups, only sales were rationalised; fellow-members continued to compete against each other in a weak market. Presto absorbed Dux (another conservative and impoverished German house) in 1926, and were absorbed in their turn by N.A.G. a year later. Their last effort, a 2·6-litre pushrod six with light-alloy pistons, survived for a while longer under the N.A.G.-Presto name.

14 ZÜST 25–35 h.p., 1913, Italy

The Swiss-born Ing. Roberto Züst became a partner in the Güller and Groff engineering firm in 1871, and took over as sole owner in 1893. Four years later experimental work on motor-cars was set in train by his five sons, serious manufacture beginning in 1902. Early Züsts, such as the car with which Antonio Scarfoglio took third place in the New York–Paris race of 1908, were in the classical Mercedes idiom favoured by the majority of Italian manufacturers, though from 1906 onward there were also some modest 3- and 4-cylinder shaft-driven machines made in a separate factory under the name of Brixia-Züst. These were widely used as taxicabs.

The Agadir Crisis of 1907 played havoc with the under-capitalised Italian industry, dependent as it was on luxury-car exports, and though Züst continued to produce chain-driven giants —a vast 50–60 h.p. S.235 or *Tipo America* with dual ignition was still quoted at $5,000 in New York in

1911/12, and remained in the catalogue as late as 1915—they followed FIAT's lead with smaller offerings featuring L-head monobloc engines and bevel drive.

Typical of these was the 4·7-litre S305 with compensated rod-operated brakes on the rear wheels (there was no transmission brake) and a top speed of 60–65 m.p.h. The English concessionaire was Enrico Bertelli, later to be responsible for coachwork on the Aston Martins designed by his brother Augusto Cesare. Like FIAT and Isotta Fraschini, Züst offered their clientele a choice of radiator shapes. The traditional mock-Mercedes style was usually found on smaller and cheaper models, like the 2,853 c.c. 15–25 h.p., the FIAT-like pear-shape being used for the 25–35 and the bigger, but generally similar 6·2-litre 35–50. The wire wheels, another Züst option, were British-made, by Riley of Coventry.

In 1918 the Züst concern was acquired by the Officine Mecchaniche of Milan, a firm of locomotive and streetcar builders. The bigger and smaller type disappeared, but the S305 acquired a new lease of life under the O.M. name, surviving until 1922, when it was phased out in favour of Barratouché's four- and six-cylinder side-valve designs.

15 GRÄF *UND* STIFT 40/45 PS, 1913, Austria

'The Rolls-Royce of Austria' is, curiously, little known outside its homeland, largely because its makers seldom bothered with competitions, if one excepts the unsuccessful entry of a single 8-litre car in the 1907 Kaiserpreis.

The firm's beginnings were modest. Between 1895 and 1897 the Gräf brothers experimented with a De Dion-engined f.w.d. *voiturette*, before passing on to manufacture cars for Arnold Spitz, a Viennese automobile agent. This connection was severed in 1907, whereupon they concentrated on large and luxurious vehicles with side valves in a T-head, Friedmann-type splash lubrication, leather cone clutches, four forward speeds, and surprisingly, shaft drive. Initially low-tension ignition was used, but by 1909 this had given way to a high-tension magneto. Smallest of the range was the 4·2-litre 16/22 PS, but for those requiring more urge there were the 5·9-litre 18/32, which would exceed 50 m.p.h., and the huge 40/45 with a 7·3-litre engine developing 50 b.h.p. at a gentle 1,500 r.p.m. A tourer weighed 5,465 pounds, in spite of which more than 60 m.p.h. was possible. A five-bearing crankshaft, a de Dion rear axle, and a water-cooled transmission brake featured in the specification. In 1914 Gräf *und* Stift adopted the fashionable vee-radiator.

In this year a 40/45 was delivered to the Emperor Franz Josef II, and it was in this vehicle that the last of the Hapsburgs, Karl, fled with his Empress to Switzerland in 1918. More famous, however, was the 18/32 acquired by Graf von Harrach in 1911, in which the Archduke Franz Ferdinand was assassinated at Sarajevo on 28 June, 1914. It is now on display in Vienna's Army Museum.

Gräf *und* Stift continued to make passenger cars until 1938, when the last of their magnificent 5·9-litre o.h.c. straight-eights was delivered. Sadly, however, the silver lion mascot had already found its way on to lesser vehicles, in the shape of licence-produced 15CV Citroëns and Ford V8s.

16 FISCHER 10/33 CV, 1913, Switzerland

Most of Switzerland's great automobile engineers preferred to seek their fortunes abroad, in view of the local motorphobia that prevailed until the 1920s. Martin Fischer, however, stayed at home. As early as 1904 he had startled the boulevardiers of his native Zurich with an astonishing air-cooled monocar. Its single chain drive was ordinary enough, but Fischer used pedal-operated steering, the driver's hands being employed for braking and gear-changing, while the petrol tank doubled as his seat. This prentice effort evolved into the friction-drive Turicum, an otherwise conventional motorcar which was made until 1914, but in 1908 the restless Fischer formed a new company, making some 70 machines with friction-and-chain transmission before turning to a conventional 2½-litre four.

His next effort was, however, more advanced, for beneath an orthodox exterior the five-bearing four-cylinder 10/33 CV concealed a single-sleeve-valve layout in which both inlets and exhausts were actuated by half-moon-shaped slides. The four-speed gearbox contained four concentric, internally toothed rings (commemorated on the firm's radiator emblem), and the cars rode on Fischer's own patent quick-detachable wheels. A prototype tested over 2,500 miles was said to have used 22 per cent less fuel than a comparable poppet-valve, though no exact figures were published. Contemporary reports were sceptical of the Fischer crescent-valve—understandably, since the Darracq and Itala rotary-valve engines had given endless trouble—but cars were sold in Germany, England, and Brazil, and about 180 10/33s were made, plus two prototype 4·1-litre sixes. The War put a stop to the company's operations.

Licences were also sold abroad. Delaugère-Clayette of France exhibited a Fischer-engined car at the 1913 Paris Salon, and Withers of London offered something called a Magic which was either a native Fischer or a Delaugère. The American licencees, Palmer-Singer, marketed their elegant vee-radiatored 6L in 1913, but it is significant that at the end of the year they were feverishly promoting their '1915' range, and most of these cars had conventional poppet-valve engines by Herschell-Spillman. One may even suspect a connection between the Fischer engine and Palmer-Singer's subsequent bankruptcy.

17 DETROIT ELECTRIC, 1914, 1918, U.S.A.

Electric cars still enjoyed a considerable popularity in America as late as 1914, when 21 different makes were quoted. The interesting thing about the Detroit is that it soldiered on until 1941. By this time, of course, the firm was a pale shadow of its former self. In 1910

1,500-odd Detroit Electrics found buyers, and even in 1915 the Anderson Electric Car Company found it worth their while to hire an attractive red-headed teenager to demonstrate the latest models, but a quarter of a century later they were lucky if they sold a dozen vehicles in a year. A large order from the Spanish Government in 1938 had to be refused through sheer lack of surviving facilities. A conservative clientele had little interest in new types, and no need for them either, since electrics never wore out.

The Detroit's series-wound motor was hung in the centre of the chassis and drove direct to a differential back axle: its output of 3 b.h.p. was sufficient to propel the car on level roads at 25 m.p.h. Steering was by lever, and the batteries were stowed in compartments at front and rear. 125 miles between charges were claimed, and in 1908 a Detroit was driven from Washington to Baltimore and back on a single charge, but such economy demanded a leisurely gait.

After 1914 only closed bodies were offered; pneumatics were standardised in 1918, and a year later cars were available with wheel steering and dummy bonnets, initially aping the Franklin, but later modelled on Willys or Dodge—the combination of the latter's 1936 grille and the traditional china-cabinet bodywork was most infelicitous. Prices were high, as befitted a clientele that embraced Henry Ford and Thomas A. Edison—around $2,800 (£560) in 1914. In 1913 a company was formed to build Detroits in Britain, and an anglicised example of the breed appeared on the Arrol-Johnston stand at Olympia that year. It was driven down from Dumfries under its own power, but even running costs quoted at a farthing per mile could not make Britons electricity minded.

18 IMP, 1914, U.S.A.

One of the best-known American cyclecars was the Imp, made by McIntyre of Auburn, Indiana, already known for their high-wheelers. It was conceived in the Bédélia idiom with final drive by long belts from a countershaft; the friction primary drive gave four forward speeds and a reverse. The engine was an air-cooled vee-twin, steering was by cable-and-bobbin, and the main unitary structure was of wood. Advanced for the period was the all-independent suspension, while the use of coil ignition enabled the makers to provide electric lighting —this was an extra at the American list price of $375 (£75), but inclusive for Britons, who paid £98.

A handle protruding from the steering-wheel boss actuated a mechanical starter, and the Imp, like the Woods-Mobilette, was long and narrow, with a wheelbase of 100 inches and a track of a mere three feet, necessitating tandem seating. The driver's seat was adjustable, and the passenger was said to have ample leg-room. Technical journalists were unconvinced. One critic, commenting on claims that such vehicles could be stowed in the front halls of apartment blocks, wrote that 'doorways of sheds or barns are usually wide enough, and certainly any man who could afford to pay $350 for such an outfit could afford another $10 to widen his gate'!

On 15 b.h.p. the Imp would do 50 m.p.h., and its sponsors planned to produce 40,000 a year. In March, 1914, they spoke of orders for 10,000 on hand, half that quantity being destined for Britain, already well supplied with native cyclecars. Nothing, however, was heard of the Imp after 1914, and a year later the McIntyre car also ceased production.

19 MAXWELL 50–6, 1914, U.S.A.

While Europe had had enough of sixes for sixes' sake by 1914, America was discovering the joys of smooth, flexible power, and a 3–50 m.p.h. range in direct drive.

Not, of course, that everyone fell for such blandishments. Henry Ford, disillusioned by his skirmish with the expensive Model-K in 1905, refused to make any kind of six again until 1941, Willys-Overland's early sixes were spasmodic and few in number, and Dodge shot straight into the best-selling league on a one-model programme—that model was, of course, a four. The same normally went for the Maxwell, sole survivor of that infelicitous consortium, the United States Motor Company, which had collapsed in 1912. When the *marque* was salvaged from the ruins, their old-established Messenger flat-twin was dropped, and the factory's efforts concentrated on a conventional side-valve four, the Model-25. This policy paid off: 17,000 Maxwells were sold in 1913, and the company reached its peak in 1917, with 75,000 units delivered.

This makes it all the more surprising that Maxwell entered the six-cylinder stakes with a big tourer on a 130-inch wheelbase so soon after the *débâcle* of 1912. It rode on 36-inch wooden wheels, and it came complete with dual ignition and a Gray and Davis electric starter. Unfortunately, it was no bargain, at a list price of $2,350 (£470); at this figure it was undercut, not only by the big battalions (Buick, Jeffery, Oakland, and Studebaker) but also by the large and luxurious 6–54 Hudson, which offered seven-passenger bodywork for $100 less. For all its designation, too, the six-cylinder Maxwell disposed of only 41 b.h.p. Buyers had the choice of left or right-hand steering.

The model lasted only a couple of seasons: thereafter Maxwell reverted to a fours-only policy which persisted until W. Chrysler killed the *marque* in 1925, replacing it with a similar cheap car bearing his own name.

20 TRUMBULL, 1914, U.S.A.

Well above the cyclecar class was the Connecticut-built Trumbull. Unlike its contemporary, the Saxon, it was aimed largely at foreign markets, and about 1,500 of the 2,000 cars manufactured went abroad, over 300 of these to Australia.

A simple little machine on an 80-inch wheelbase, the Trumbull was powered by a two-bearing side-valve four-cylinder engine made by the Hermann Manufacturing Co. of Detroit. Ignition was by magneto, and suspension was of Ford type, with transverse leaf springs at front and rear. The first 300 cars had friction-and-chain drive, but this was found unsatisfactory on bad roads, and subsequent Trumbulls used a three-speed gearbox in unit with the back axle. Gear and brake levers were central, the clutch was a leather cone, all brakes worked on the rear wheels, and steering was by rack and pinion. Prices were modest—$425 (£85) for a roadster, and $600 for a coupé. All cars came equipped with electric lights and horn and, surprisingly, quick-detachable wire wheels, but a spare wheel cost an extra $25, a speedometer $20, and a Ward-Leonard electric starter $75.

The 60 m.p.h. speedometer, incidentally, was no idle joke, for the 950-pound Trumbull would exceed 50 in favourable circumstances, and fuel consumption was a modest 30 m.p.g. The car sold for £105 in England, where it aroused favourable press comment, though unfortunately the engine's 18 brake horses were too much for the transmission, and broken half-shafts were not unknown.

Though the United States stayed neutral until 1917, the Trumbull was none the less a war casualty, since hostilities cut it off from the markets in which it was fast establishing itself. The last straw came when I. B. Trumbull, one of the brothers behind the company, was drowned in the wreck of the *Lusitania* in May, 1915.

21 G.W.K., 1914, Great Britain

Its sponsors always denied that the G.W.K. was a cyclecar, despite its 1,100 c.c. twin-cylinder engine and friction transmission.

The prototype was put together by Arthur Grice, J. T. Wood, and C. M. Keiller in a stable at Beckenham in 1911, using a vertical-twin Coventry-Simplex marine engine, a De Dion-type tubular radiator, and Chater-Lea wire wheels and front axle. Production started later in the year at Datchet. The engine was mounted behind the seats, and its flywheel served as a driving disc which engaged (at right angles) with a fibre- or cork-faced driven disc. This was arranged to slide across the flywheel, its four notches giving the four 'gears'. The clutch mechanism engaged one end of the driven-disc shaft, and the other end drove by shaft to an orthodox differential back axle. The G.W.K.'s conventional controls were matched by a fairly conventional appearance; the radiator lived at the front at the end of a short bonnet.

The system worked well as long as the drive-shaft was kept short, and on a chassis weight of 730 pounds the G.W.K. was capable of about 45 m.p.h. Servicing was cheap and easy. The fibre facings on the driven disc had a life of 10,000 miles, and linoleum could be used in an emergency, while slip and 'flats' were seldom problems as long as the machinery was kept grease-free and the clutch used with respect. 1,069 of the GW.K. twins were made up to 1915, and another hundred in 1919–20.

Unfortunately, after the wartime move to the legendary 'Jam Factory' at Maidenhead (originally G.W.K.'s body shop) they tried to make a small touring car, the front-engined F-type with 1,368 c.c. four-cylinder engine. This suffered from transmission whip, while the driven disc made unpleasant ringing noises. G.W.K. struggled on until 1931, with abortive attempts to revive the rear-engined recipe. The Model-J of 1922 had a conventional bonnet, but at the end Grice tried mounting his engine (either the Coventry-Climax four or a Coventry-Victor flat-twin) over the rear axle. Nobody, however, wanted friction drive any more.

22 MENDIP 11 h.p., 1914, Great Britain

Small engineering firms could still make cars economically in 1914, but it is surprising to find a light car emanating from a modest village in the Mendips, even if G. W. Harris's concern dated back to 1810, had its own foundry and forge, and had already built a number of steam- and petrol-engined lorries for local clients. It is even more surprising that the Mendip car engine designed by W. L. Adams was made in its entirety at Chewton Mendip, with the exception of the block and crankshaft imported from Belgium. What is more, this little T-headed affair had been put on the market as a proprietary unit in October 1913, a good six months before the first 11 h.p. Mendip was announced—it was sold complete with its Manchester-built clutch and three-speed gearbox. Mendip fabricated their own frames from Belgian steel; they were also responsible for the two-seater coachwork.

Features of the car were a bullnose radiator in the Morris or A.C. idiom, a footbrake working in internal-expanding shoes on the rear wheels, and an overhead worm back axle. Provision was made for the installation of a lighting dynamo, but pre-War Mendips were not electrically equipped. During the War the firm undertook sub-contract work on Straker-Squire lorries. Harris, incidentally, had sold out to W. H. Bateman Hope in 1913, and subsequently put together a few Mendip-type cars in Weston-super-Mare.

In 1919 operations were transferred to a new factory at Bristol, and a few cars of pre-War type were assembled from parts on hand. Since blocks were no longer obtainable from Belgium the firm adopted the British Alpha engine, and in March it was announced that a batch of a hundred new Mendips was being erected. Post-War inflation, alas, took its toll: the price was up from its 1914 level of £157 10s to nearly £300, and when Hope died the business closed down. Though a new company formed at Melksham apparently built no more cars, over 300 had been produced at Chewton and Bristol.

23 ADLER 5/13 PS MODELL-K, 1914, Germany

The big-car-in-miniature theme was not confined to Britain: in Germany Adler, Dürkopp, N.A.G. and Wanderer offered some excellent light fours.

Heinrich Kleyer had been making Adler bicycles at Frankfurt-am-Main since 1886, and had also produced wheels for Karl Benz. In 1899 he started to build de Dion tricycles under licence, and 1900 saw a single-cylinder light car which was uncommonly close

to the contemporary Renault. The first of a line of successful fours followed in 1904, and by the time the 5/13 PS came on the market Adler had already made their name with a modest 6/14 PS, and its development, the 8/15 PS of 1,767 c.c.

On the first Ks the cylinders were pair-cast, but in 1912 a monobloc unit was adopted, developing 13 b.h.p. at 1,500 r.p.m. It was pressure-lubricated with thermo-syphon circulation, and Adler's own carburetter incorporated a hot-spot. The clutch was a leather-faced cone, and buyers had the choice of tandem or side-by-side seating. For those in quest of something roomier, the enlarged 1½-litre 6/16 PS, or KL, joined the range in 1913.

Unlike many of its German contemporaries, the Adler was well-proportioned, wearing a more rounded edition of the traditional rectangular radiator. The dash was of cast aluminium, and cars sold in England, at any rate, came complete with an eagle mascot, which probably helped to justify the high asking price of £298 ($1,490). Though its makers claimed only 40 m.p.h., the K would do 50 on its 4·1:1 top gear, with a useful 30 available on second. Weight was not excessive at 1,120 pounds, and quite a few found buyers in Britain as 'Morgan-Adler "Carettes"' (At the outbreak of War the unsold stock was hurriedly stripped of badges and sold off as plain 'Morgans'!). The 5/13 PS was revived in 1919 with a more powerful 14 b.h.p. engine, but both it and the companion 6/16 were replaced in 1921 by an ugly little 6/22 PS with vee-radiator and (a retrograde step) side valves in a T-head.

24 BERGMANN-METALLURGIQUE 10/30 PS, 1914, 1922, Germany

The vee-radiator—contemporary English reports, incidentally, never called it anything but a 'wedge'—was no German invention. It was inspired by that admirable Belgian car, the Métallurgique, which had been so equipped since 1907.

While most Belgian makers looked westwards to Britain for sales, Métallurgique had had a German agency in Cologne since 1905, and four years later the big Bergmann electrical concern (which had a financial interest in Métallurgique) abandoned their own electric and petrol cars in favour of a licence agreement with the Marchienne-au-Pont factory. Technically the new Bergmann-Métallurgiques were identical with the Belgian product, and at first the majority of components was imported. By 1914, however, everything, the bodies included, was of German origin, which was a pity, since Métallurgiques were renowned for the elegance of their Vanden Plas coachwork. A good deal of design work was also undertaken by Bergmann, under Ernst Lehmann and Sidney Smith, who had joined the company from Napiers in 1909. The German factory was in fact responsible for the superb 27–80 h.p. Prince Henry model, a formidable performer with a plated-brass crankcase which would top 80 m.p.h.

The standard article as produced in Marchienne and Berlin alike had, however, side-by-side valves. It was also invariably a four, and in addition to the 10/30 the German range embraced a 1·6-litre 6/19 PS, a 3·1-litre 12/35 PS, a 3½-litre 14/40 PS, and a big 29/70 of 7·3 litres' capacity which was good for 70 m.p.h. Specifications were straightforward, with fixed heads, three-bearing crankshafts, full-pressure lubrication, thermo-syphon circulation, and cone clutches. After the War the 10/30 became the staple model, now with full electrics and Autovac feed, though at the very end, in 1921–22, Bergmann essayed something that the parent company had never contemplated—a six-cylinder car.

25 DIXI R.12 10/26 PS, 1914, Germany

The Dixi story goes back to 1898, when Heinrich Ehrhardt made some electric cars at Eisenach under the Wartburg name, later producing the French Decauville *voiturette* under licence in 3 h.p. and 5 h.p. sizes. A Decauville-inspired four followed in 1902, but after Ehrhardt sold his motor-car interests in 1904, the name of the product was changed to Dixi ('I have spoken', or, figuratively, 'It's the last word'), and the factory switched to all-German creations from the drawing-board of Willy Seck.

Most Dixis were modest enough vehicles, though at the head of the 1914 range there was still a 26/40 PS U-type with side valves in a T-head and a capacity of 6·8 litres. The R.12, however, is much more typical of their thinking, and derived from the 1·6-litre 6/14 PS which distinguished itself in the 1909 *Rund um* Berlin and the 1910 Eisenach *Sternfahrt*. Fitted with a lightened body, one of these cars recorded 103 km/h. (64 m.p.h.) over the flying kilometre at Frankfurt Speed Trials. In 1910 Dixi built some 2·1-litre machines with tulip-shaped body-work and monobloc engines for the Prince Henry Trials, but though these proved most efficient, attaining 60 m.p.h. on 32 b.h.p., and would run up to 2,400 r.p.m., they were over-whelmed by the Austro-Daimlers and Benz. Whatever the formula, it seldom paid to build small in the German rallies of the period.

The 10/26 represents the norm in German touring-car design, with side valves in a L-head, pressure lubrication, pump and fan cooling, a leather cone clutch, and a four-speed separate gear-box. The three-quarter-elliptic rear suspension and fixed wooden wheels with detachable rims are typical of the period.

In 1927 Dixi acquired a licence to build Austin Sevens in Germany, and two years later the company was acquired by B.M.W. of Munich. The Wartburg name has been twice revived, once for a sports edition of the German Austin, and subsequently in 1956 for a D.K.W. derivative made in the old Eisenach works by the East German Government.

26 WANDERER 5/12 PS,
1914, 5/15 PS, 1918,
Germany

The little Wanderer was one of the K-model Adler's competitors. It also came from a former bicycle maker, who had been in business at Chemnitz, Saxony, since 1885. Motorcycles were added to the repertoire in 1902, and a

prototype twin-cylinder light car was tested in 1905, followed by a four two years later. In 1911 J. B. Winkelhofer of Wanderer was approached by Ettore Bugatti, who hoped to sell them what later became the 'Bébé' Peugeot, but by this time their own development programme was well advanced, and in 1912 the 5/12 PS went into pro-duction.

Like the Adler, it was a small mono-bloc four with three-speed gearbox, tandem seating, bevel drive, and dif-ferential back axle, but that is as far as the resemblance went. Wanderer pre-ferred overhead inlet valves, though their 1,145 c.c. power unit developed only an average 12 b.h.p. The wire wheels came with detachable rims, there was full-pressure lubrication (with an oil-pressure gauge on the dash), and the clutch was a leather-to-metal cone, mounted, with its gearbox, in unit with the engine. Extensive tests included a 2,000-kilometre workout in the Tyrol and the Dolomites, from which the Wanderer emerged without trouble. Two cars were also entered for the 1914 Austrian Alpine Trials, in which they were the smallest contestants with the exception of an 1,100 c.c. Singer Ten: one of them retired.

On a weight of 1,425 pounds the 5/12 PS would do nearly 50 m.p.h., and it was well-liked, acquiring the sobriquet of 'Püppchen' (doll). By 1914 a more powerful 5/15 PS with full overhead valves, a capacity of 1,220 c.c., and a longer wheelbase of 94½ inches had made its appearance. This came in tandem or 'sociable' versions, though German army officers preferred the former species, since they could sit in seclusion in the back, immune from the gossip of chatty drivers. The theme was continued until 1925, later cars having 20 b.h.p. engines and detachable cylinder heads, while a 1,500 c.c. sports version developed as much as 40 b.h.p.

27 ISOTTA FRASCHINI OC5, 1914–15, Italy

Isotta Fraschinis of the immediate pre-World War I period are indelibly associated in the enthusiast's mind with overhead camshafts and four-wheel brakes, though in fact this combination was found only on the big 70–80 h.p. TM-type, and its stablemate the chain-driven KM of over ten litres' capacity. Though all the Isottas shown at the 1913 Paris Salon had front-wheel brakes, some of the smaller species, like the 2·3-litre FC, were still being made with the old arrangements.

Isotta, in any case, were still recovering from the near-collapse that followed the Agadir Crisis. In 1907 they ranked second only to FIAT in the Italian motor industry and employed 1,400 hands: a year later financial stringency had driven them into the arms of Lorraine-Dietrich of France. Independence was soon regained, and by 1909 they were exporting 75 per cent of their output, and so far from acting as a sub-division of a French firm, they had actually sold a manufacturing licence to Praga in Austria-Hungary.

Fraschini's four-wheel brakes, unlike Argyll's, were uncoupled; the pedal took care of the rear wheels and the lever of the front, which meant that both had to be applied simultaneously

to ensure freedom from side-slip. In other respects the OC5 was entirely conventional, with side-valve monobloc engine, which was fairly expensive (it cost £40 more in chassis form than FIAT's comparable *Tipo* 3 of like capacity) and also generously dimensioned; the shorter of the two available wheelbases was 124½ inches. Traditionalists could specify side-chain drive, and by 1914 dynamo lighting was standard equipment.

As to radiator shape, this was an era of 'no holds barred' and at least four different styles were found on 1914 Isottas. On the touring models, however, the choice paralleled the ideas of FIAT and Züst on the subject. The smaller species were usually seen with something in the mock Mercedes idiom, while for larger cars a pear-shape was the recognised wear.

28 LANCIA THETA, 1914, Italy

Vincenzo Lancia's company enjoys the reputation of never having made a bad car. Curiously, FIAT's former star driver made no racing models himself, preferring to concentrate on touring types of above-average sophistication. Between 1907 and 1913 he made about 1,700 cars; by the time the Theta gave way to the Kappa in 1919 this figure had been doubled.

In Italy, great minds thought alike, and there are marked similarities between the 1914 offerings of FIAT, Isotta, and Lancia, though the latter had been using monobloc engines since 1909, and his 1913 model, the 4·1-litre Delta, boasted a respectable 45 b.h.p.

Further, the list price of £750 ($3,750) included dynamo lighting. Lancia's prosperity was reflected in sales to Argentina, Australia, Ceylon, Cuba, France, the Netherlands, India, Malaya, Morocco, New Zealand, Rumania, Russia, South Africa, Switzerland, and the U.S.A.

The Theta's specification embraced full-pressure lubrication, a four-speed unit gearbox, and a dry multi-disc clutch, and output was 70 b.h.p. at 2,200 r.p.m., which gave it a brisk performance on a 3·26:1 axle ratio. Lancia also shares with Hispano-Suiza the distinction of introducing electric starters to Europe, and the pedal-operated Rushmore unit was standard equipment on all Thetas. Equally advanced was the layout of the switches: not only the ignition, but also the lamps, the electric klaxon, and the panel light were controlled from the steering-wheel, while the steering-column was adjustable for rake.

Theta-derivatives saw extensive war service, being adopted by the Royal Naval Air Service, and also by the Ulster Constabulary—a number of armoured Lancia lorries of 1916–18 vintage were still on charge in Belfast in the late 'fifties. The design was modernised in 1919, emerging as the Kappa model, still with side-by-side valves and transmission brake, but with output increased to 90 b.h.p. and central gear and brake levers. King George VI (then the Duke of York) owned a Kappa tourer. Last of the Lancias with in-line engine was the o.h.v. Dikappa of 1922, but the advanced vee-four Lambda had already gone into production, and the final Theta derivative had a short run.

29 SCANIA-VABIS 22 h.p., 1914, Sweden

Sweden's emergence as a major car-making nation is almost a phenomenon of the 1960s. As late as the 1930s Volvo's average annual output was around 5,000 units, while back in pre-1914 days the combination of poor roads, a hard winter, and an economy that militated against a large moneyed class kept the home market small. Such native makers as there were (Scania, Tidaholm, and Vabis) concentrated on commercial vehicles, and Swedish motorists relied on foreign imports, initially German and later American. This early preference for German cars explains the Teutonic appearance and specification of the solidly-built Scania-Vabis, which could be mistaken for a contemporary Horch with its fixed wooden wheels and three-quarter elliptic rear springs. Some features were, however, peculiarly Swedish; the bigger 4½-litre Scanias had a special underdrive incorporated in the back axle for dealing with snowbound roads.

Scania-Vabis (today associated with SAAB) was a fusion of two erstwhile rivals, Vagnfabriken of Södertalje and Scania of Malmö. The former concern was experimenting with a V4 hot-air engine in 1897, though its first prototype car used a flat-twin unit. Scania, by contrast, began their career by manufacturing Humber cycles under licence, progressing in 1901 to a chain-driven car powered by a twin-cylinder Kamper engine of German origin. By 1905 they were using Wentzel-designed o.h.v. units. At the 1903 Stockholm Show they earned themselves some useful publicity by driving one of their exhibits the 650 kilometres from Malmö. Even after the merger in 1911, production was continued in both factories for thirteen years before operations were concentrated on Södertalje, where the works still are.

Trucks were always the firm's main interest, though smaller models were based on the 4½-litre passenger-car chassis; total production of 'pleasure' vehicles between 1906 and 1924 amounted to a mere 485 units. After the closure of the Malmö works it ceased altogether, with the exception of a brace of 2·3-litre four-cylinder sedans on American lines made to special order in 1929—one of these is preserved in the works museum.

30 F.N. 1250, 1914, Belgium

Belgium's motor industry was export-oriented; more specifically, it was British-oriented, the United Kingdom accounting for more than a third of foreign sales. Thus large and expensive machinery predominated.

The principal exception to this philosophy was the Fabrique Nationale d'Armes de Guerre. As one of Europe's biggest ordnance factories they could afford to dispense with automobiles, and did so after 1935. Their daily output in 1908—when their car business was firmly established—was 1,700 assorted firearms, 400,000 cartridges, 1,500 bicycles, 50 motorcycles—and only about 3,600 F.N.'s had been made when War broke out in 1914; a goodly proportion of these were the well-loved 1400 and 1600 types with four pair-cast cylinders, thermo-syphon circulation, three- (and later four-) speed gearboxes and shaft

drive, which sold for £285 ($1,425) in England.

The 1250 first seen at the 1913 Paris Salon was something altogether smaller, representing F.N.'s answer to Singer, Calcott, and Adler. Its monobloc engine with trough-and-dipper lubrication was entirely orthodox, though pressure feed from a rear tank was unusual on a light car, and there was a three-bearing crankshaft. The detachable wooden wheels were of F.N.'s own make, the clutch was a leather cone, and three forward speeds sufficed. More interesting, the 1250 boasted a mechanical starter, the manufacturers dispensing with a starting handle. It was supplied complete as a two-seater: a bare chassis was not listed.

The War prevented any large-scale production, but as early as May 1919 it was back on the market with a higher radiator and a longer, 105½-inch wheelbase. In spite of the added weight the post-War 1250A and 1250T models were quite good performers, cruising at an easy 35–40 m.p.h., with excellent roadholding and direct, high-geared steering; the cone clutches were notoriously fierce. As late as 1923 the company introduced another variation on the 1914 theme, the 1,328 c.c. 1250N, still with fixed head and foot transmission brake. A year later this was dropped in favour of a modern small four, the o.h.v. 1300 with four-wheel brakes.

31 RUSSELL-KNIGHT 28, 1914, Canada

Canada has never really needed a motor industry: Detroit lies very conveniently 'over the water'. Hence most Canadian cars have been special versions of existing American themes adapted to meet either local conditions or that curious Commonwealth patriotism which regarded Buicks and Chevrolets as entirely acceptable as long as they were 'built in the British Empire'.

The Russell was perhaps the best known and most successful of the native breeds, enjoying an eleven-year run from 1905, though as early as 1900 the Canada Cycle and Motor Company were selling De Dion-type Quads. They subsequently made the Ivanhoe electric car, and became Ford's first Canadian agent. The 1905 Russells had 16 h.p. flat-twin engines in the best American tradition, though these lived under the hood rather than under the floor, and drove the rear wheels by shaft and bevel. Four-cylinder models followed in 1907, and the first Russell-Knight in 1910, Tom Russell having acquired the exclusive Canadian rights for the Knight and Kilbourne sleeve-valve patents. So exclusive were they that they barred John N. Willys from selling his American Knights across the border.

Russell built 'up to a standard and not down to a price', which explains why his first sleeve-valve cars retailed at a re-sounding $5,000 (£1,000), putting them in the Packard or Locomobile category. Poppet-valve models were, however, still made, and they were marketed with electric self-starters as early as 1912. 1913 Russells conformed to the prevailing American formula, with unit gearboxes, left-hand drive, and central control, but standard equipment included a rear-seat windshield and a power tyre pump. A year later a certain cheapening was detectable: alongside the Knight at $2,975 there was $1,475-worth of Light Six, powered by the familiar side-valve Continental engine.

Ironically, however, it was not to be American competition that killed the Russell: it was patriotism. In 1916 the directors decided to devote their whole energies to the production of aero-engines for the Allies. Willys snapped up the Canadian Knight rights, and the *marque* was not revived after the Armistice.

32 BREWSTER, 1915, 1919, U.S.A.

Many coachbuilders have turned to car manufacture. The outstanding modern examples are, of course, Jensen and S.S. (Jaguar), but Brewster and Co. of Long Island City had a far longer record, having been a hallowed name in the carriage-building world for over a century. They were to earn an equal degree of respect for their custom bodies on such chassis as Packard and Rolls-Royce.

The Brewster car, however, was relatively little known. During its ten-year run probably no more than two hundred were made, and most of these were chauffeur-driven town carriages with designations like 'double enclosed drive' and 'glass quarter brougham'. Despite their unusual oval radiators they lacked elegance, due more than anything to the short wheelbase of 125 inches.

Mechanical specification changed little, and all Brewsters used the same $4\frac{1}{2}$-litre four-cylinder Knight sleeve-valve engine with detachable head, magneto ignition, pressure lubrication, and pump cooling. The clutch was a cone, three forward speeds sufficed, the cantilever rear suspension assured a smooth ride, and all brakes were on the rear wheels. Full electrics were standard from the start, though Brewster, unusually, preferred a 12-volt system, and closed bodies featured the company's patented double windshield. A few open styles were offered up to 1918–19, these including a 1917 roadster featuring not only a dickey (rumble) seat, but also a precarious auxiliary perch for an extra passenger atop the toolbox on the right-hand running board. Prices were always expensive: in 1918 formal-bodied types listed at $8,300 (£1,660), inflated three years later to a formidable $10,500 (£2,100). Production ceased in 1925, when Brewster merged with Rolls-Royce of America Inc., and concentrated their efforts on bodies for the Springfield-built cars. There was, however, a brief comeback in 1934–36 with some elegant vehicles based on lengthened Ford V8 chassis. These had unusual heart-shape grilles echoing the original Brewsters, flared wings, and double front bumpers. Most were town cars, but a few phaetons and convertibles were made.

33 DODGE BROTHERS' FOUR, 1915, U.S.A.

John and Horace Dodge ran a machine-shop in Detroit which was responsible for Henry Ford's first engines, and their one-tenth share in his company was to make them multi-millionaires.

Equally successful was their own car,

launched in November 1914. Initially the Dodge factory employed 48 workers: fourteen years later the pay-roll was 35,000. In its first full year of production—1915—the Dodge was outsold only by Ford and Willys-Overland, and in the ensuing decade it never fell below sixth place. By October, 1920, Dodge Bros. were making 625 cars a day.

The Dodge Four was the company's staple until mid-1927. In original guise it used a slow-running 25 b.h.p. $3\frac{1}{2}$-litre side-valve engine, mounted in unit with a three-speed gearbox and cone clutch. Left-hand drive was, of course, standard, and all brakes were on the rear wheels. It was modestly priced at $785 (£157).

There were some individual features. Pre-1918 Dodges had magneto ignition, the firm preferred 12-volt electrics to the customary 6-volt system, and pre-1926 cars were noted for their 'back-to-front' gear change with the two higher ratios on the left of the 'gate'. Their toughness was proverbial. In 1916 General Pershing took some Dodges on his punitive expedition against Pancho Villa in Mexico, and found them so reliable that the *marque* was adopted as standard army transport, serving as ambulance and Signal Corps truck as well as staff car. Until very recent years Dodge Fours were frequently seen working as garage tow-trucks in Australia.

Up to the middle 'twenties there were few major changes. A lengthened wheelbase, larger brake drums, and a multi-disc clutch came in 1916, slanting windshields in 1920, and all-steel closed bodies (which accounted for 35 per cent of sales) were standardised in 1922.

There was extensive restyling in 1924, and at long last in 1926 the Dodge acquired 6-volt electrics and a standard gear-shift. The passenger-car line was dropped in 1928 (apart from an abortive attempt at revival with the export-only DM-type of 1932), but light trucks with four-cylinder engines persisted until 1933, they being popular for newspaper-delivery work in London.

34 PIERCE-ARROW 48, 1915, U.S.A.

George Pierce started by making bird-cages, progressing to bicycles in 1892, and to a De Dion-inspired, rear-engined light car, the Pierce Motorette, in 1901. By 1903 his firm was making a 15 h.p. front-engined vertical-twin which it called the Arrow; thus logically their 24–28 h.p. four on European lines introduced later in the season became the Pierce Great Arrow. The arrow trademark (commemorated in later years by an archer mascot) became part of the company's corporate name in 1909.

By 1913 Pierce-Arrow had settled down to a three-model luxury-car range, of which the smallest type was the 38, a 4½-litre six weighing 4,200 pounds. The 8·6-litre 48 was the inter-mediate version, and at the top was the 66, a 13 litre behemoth of which it was said that 'the sensation of power con-trolled by the throttle is very much allied to that of handling a hydraulic lift'—which meant 70-plus m.p.h. on a 2-to-1 top gear, at the price of an insatiable thirst for fuel and tyres. The 48 was the same thing slightly scaled

down, and from 1913 onwards the electric headlamps were faired into the front fenders, a Pierce hallmark though it was never compulsory. Initially starting was by compressed air, but 1914 models came with full electrics and power tyre pumps, and weight was up to 5,000 pounds. The cars were made to European standards; engines were dynamometer-tested, bare chassis did a 100-mile road trial, and there was a final run after the body was fitted. Changes were infrequent; double-drop frames featured in 1915, and electric clocks on the 1916 cars. The famous Dual Valve engine with its detachable head and alloy pistons came with the B5 series of 1919. By now the 48 was the staple, its bigger and smaller sisters being supplied to special order only. Conservatism was reflected in the right-hand steering, not abandoned until 1920—this was regarded as logical on cars intended for chauffeur-drive in a country with a right-hand rule of the road. Customers in 1915 had the choice of fifteen body styles, from a simple runabout at $4,900 (£980) up to a 'Vestibule Suburban Landaulet' at a resounding $6,200.

35 PACKARD TWIN-SIX, 1916, 1921, U.S.A.

The 'three Ps of America' were all still healthy in 1916, but whereas Pierce-Arrow clung to the elephantine six, and Peerless had lately essayed a vee-eight, Packard went the whole way with the world's first commercially produced twelve-cylinder. What is more, they managed to sell over 10,000 of them in the first year, and the

Twin-Six was destined to be their staple offering until 1920, when a six was reinstated in the range. When the model went on show for the first time in San Francisco, 25,000 visitors filed through the local Packard showrooms.

By luxury-car standards the Twin-Six was not very expensive, prices starting at $2,750 (£550), though post-War inflation had pushed this up to $6,000-odd by 1921. Advanced features of this 60-degree vee-twelve were full-pressure lubrication, aluminium pistons, twin water pumps, and a Lanchester vibration damper. Ignition was by coil, and three forward speeds were provided, though the Packard was so flexible that it would accelerate smoothly in top from 3 to 30 m.p.h. in 12 seconds. Output from 6·9 litres was an average 88 b.h.p., though a special lightened racing edition was persuaded to give 110 b.h.p., and top speed was in the region of 80 m.p.h. The first series came in two wheelbase lengths, 125 and 135 inches. These also differed from later Twin Sixes in having non-detachable cylinder heads, while cars made up to mid-1917 had the curious combination of left-hand drive and left-hand gear and brake levers, changed to the conventional central location on the Third Series.

Tsar Nicholas II of Russia was an early customer, though he had a standard touring car—unlike the Chinese warlord Chang Tso-Lin, who reputedly paid $35,000 for his armoured limousine in 1922. In 1921 a Twin Six made history when it conveyed Warren G. Harding to his inauguration, the first U.S. President to go to this by automobile. The twelve-cylinder Packard survived until 1923, when it gave way to a new and advanced straight-eight with four-wheel brakes. This Single Eight was the first of a line which was to persist until 1954, and the end of the company's independent existence.

36 MORRIS-COWLEY, 1916, Great Britain

W. R. Morris's 1-litre Oxford with T-head White and Poppe engine had been a great success, selling 1,400 in its first two seasons. Hence a four-seater version was a logical follow-up. Initially it was proposed to fit a version of the original power unit with a lengthened stroke, but a trip to America showed Morris that by ordering parts in batches of 3,000 he could procure a 1½-litre Continental engine (as fitted to the successful Saxon), a Detroit gearbox, an axle and steering gear for a total of £42 per car. Though the War interfered with his plans, he none the less managed to put together 1,450 of these Continental-Cowleys between 1915 and 1919. Further, this roomy family car—its wheelbase of 102 inches was a foot longer than the Oxford's—was actually cheaper than its all-British predecessor: £194 5s as against £200.

Specification was straightforward, with magneto ignition, pressure and splash lubrication, thermo-syphon cooling, a dry twin-plate clutch, and a three-speed gearbox with the usual American central ball change. All brakes were on the rear wheels, final drive was by spiral bevel, and the first Cowleys had dynamo lighting, though no starter was provided.

A stock of parts on hand enabled Morris to resume production on a small scale in 1919, but at this juncture he was forced to consider other sources of supply. Harry Ainsworth, manager of Hotchkiss's wartime ordnance plant at Coventry, offered to make him replicas of the Continental engine at a competitive price, and these Hotchkiss units went into the 1920 models, which also had Morris's sweet wet-plate clutch.

Thenceforward Morris proceeded to turn himself into Britain's number one manufacturer by slashing his prices and absorbing his component suppliers. The statistics tell their own story. Only 3,077 Morrises found buyers in 1921, but four years later sales passed the 50,000 mark. Before the immortal Bullnose faded away Mr. Morris was selling a foolproof two-seater capable of 50 m.p.h. and 30 m.p.g. for £170 ($850), inclusive of four-wheel brakes. He was a millionaire. He deserved to be.

37 BUICK SIX, 1918, U.S.A.

The Buick has an enviable reputation. Almost from its birth it has been in the best-selling league, with few disastrous years. It has also (with a few brief exceptions) adhered to pushrod-operated o.h.v. from the very first flat-twins of 1903, while a solid, middle-class clientele is reflected in such sobriquets as 'The Doctor's Friend'.

Their first six-cylinder car, the big electrically-equipped 55, appeared in 1914, and 1916 saw a big step forward, when the traditional inexpensive four

was dropped in favour of the 6–45, or Light Six, a 3·7-litre monobloc affair with splash lubrication, coil ignition, vacuum feed, three-speed box, and the usual contracting and expanding brakes on the rear wheels. Unusual was Buick's cantilever rear suspension, and initially a cone clutch was used. It was a real bargain at $985 (£197) for a touring car, though in those pre-presswork days a sedan cost nearly double the money. By 1918 capacity was up to nearly four litres, buyers had the choice of a long (124-inch) wheelbase for seven-passenger bodies, and the mass-production image was accentuated by the catalogue's observation that 'orders for special jobs are not accepted': a reasonable stipulation now that the range included two sedans and a close-coupled coupé in which the fourth passenger perched uncomfortably on a rearwards-facing 'opera seat' alongside the driver.

In those days American manufacturers tended to leave a successful car alone, and the Buick Light Six was no exception, soldiering on until 1923 with only minor changes, such as that year's drum headlights. 1919 engines had enclosed valve gear, and the hood-line was raised slightly in 1921, but that was all until 1924 brought a Packardish radiator, a detachable cylinder head, and four-wheel brakes. The record, however, speaks for itself: between 1916 and 1923 sales only twice fell below the six-figure mark—during the War in 1918, and in the slump of 1921. The cage-valve Buick Six went out in a blaze of glory with a record 201,572 deliveries in 1923, beating everyone else save Ford and Chevrolet.

38 BJERING, 1918–20, Norway

Norway had few roads, a poor population, and relatively few cars, which explains why she has been a happy hunting-ground for fanciers of Vintage American machinery until recent years. No Norwegian *marque* has ever sold in quantity, even in its homeland.

The same problems that led Scania-Vabis to build tough four-cylinder machines in Sweden prompted H. C. Bjering to devise a narrow-track vehicle capable of negotiating snow-blocked roads. He also anticipated later successful experiments in Canada and the U.S.S.R. by designing his car so that the front wheels could be replaced with skis. The first Bjering, built in 1918, was powered by an amidships-mounted air-cooled vee-four engine of Norwegian design and construction, which was mounted in a coffin-shaped unitary hull of wood. Wheelbase was 94½ inches, but track a mere 31½ inches, the rear axle was differential-less, and Ford-type transverse springing was used at both ends. Also of Ford origin were the wood wheels, shod with 30 × 3½-in. tyres, while the Bjering was a tandem-seater, the driver occupying the rear seat in the manner of the French Bédélia cyclecar. Four cars were built, successfully completing their tests on skis as well as wheels.

In 1920 Bjering came up with a revised design incorporating a rear engine, this time of in-line type, but still with o.h.v. and air cooling. Output of this unit was 20 b.h.p., and the car's construction was now of aluminium. This second Bjering performed even better than the 1918 version, passing its trials with flying colours.

Alas, for its designer's hopes, snow-clearance techniques progressed faster than car design, and the project was abandoned after only two prototypes had been built.

39 AUSTRALIAN SIX, 1918, 1920, Australia

The sensational success of the Holden—'Australia's Own Car', which sold over 170,000 units in 1970—has overshadowed earlier Australian attempts at automobile manufacture, from Thomson's 1896 steamer to the astonishing 1934 flat-four Southern Cross with automatic gearbox. Neither these nor the Buckingham, the Chic, or the Roo achieved anything, but F. H. Gordon's Australian Six was very nearly a success.

Gordon, the son of a wealthy grazier, had been in business as a car dealer in Sydney for some time before he began to import American Mitchells in 1918. His next step was to produce an Australian car, to which end he opened a new plant at Ashfield, employing 200 hands, preference being given to ex-servicemen. The first dozen Australian Sixes resembled Mitchells in style, though the disc wheels and 'Rolls-Royce' radiator of later versions suggested something far more potent—the Duesenberg-engined Roamer, then at the height of its career. The essential components—Rutenber engines, gearboxes, and back axles—came from the U.S.A., but brake rods, pedals, hoods, and bodies were locally made from Australian raw materials, and by 1920 the works were turning out one car per day.

The idea was excellent, but when one is separated from one's suppliers by an ocean, disaster can easily supervene. The engines Gordon bought were underpowered and incorrectly assembled, so that many had to be recalled for reconditioning after 5,000 miles. Australian Motors sought to anticipate the later efforts of Holden and Chrysler–Australia by shipping a small batch of cars to Singapore, but their agent never claimed them, and by the time they returned to Sydney these too needed rebuilding at their maker's expense. Between 1920 and 1930 vehicle registrations in New South Wales alone increased by 684 per cent, but by 1923 a new Chevrolet or Dodge touring car cost less than £A300 ($1,200), and the Australian Six could not compete. The company went into liquidation, and though Harkness and Hillier assembled a few more cars from parts on hand (using the more reliable Ansted engine), the venture was dead by the end of 1924.

40 MATHIS SB, 1919, 1923, France

Emile Mathis, the son of a Strasbourg hotelier, was a Frenchman by descent and a German by political circumstance, which did not prevent him from becoming Germany's biggest car dealer before the 1918 Armistice restored his chosen nationality. He had been making cars since 1910, and though some of his bigger models were thinly disguised Stoewers and Minervas, the little 958 c.c. and 1,131 c.c. Babylettes were his own work.

Between 1919 and 1930 Mathis made a serious attempt at mass-production, and at peak—in 1927—he was making over 20,000 cars a year, a figure surpassed only by Citroën and Renault. He failed just as Clyno failed in Britain, since he lacked the resources to stage an indefinite price- and model-war against Citroën.

A Heinzian variety of models poured out of the Strasbourg works, said to be the largest car factory to be housed under one roof. There were fours in profusion from the tiny 628 c.c. T-type up to the heavy 1·6-litre QM of 1929–30. Some pint-sized sixes were made between 1922 and 1926, and there was even an abortive o.h.c. straight-eight, but the SB is typical of the Mathis idiom; a simple and fairly crude machine based on his 1914 lightweights, with the addition of a differential. The fixed head, splash lubrication and angular 'military' fenders used until 1921 reflected pre-War German practice, but more modern were the electric lights and starter (standard equipment at the £520 asked in London), the absence of a transmission brake, and the four-speed box with its central ball change. Weight was 1,568 pounds, and the little Mathis would do 50 m.p.h. and 45 m.p.g., although it was rev-happy, and over-exuberant driving proved beyond the bottom end's endurance. For a while Spyker of Holland sold the SB under their name (complete with their radiator badge!) and the policy (though with a different radiator) was pursued by B.A.C. in England. From 1922 onward there was an o.h.v. edition, the SBO, but 1925 saw a move away from high-speed engines, and Mathis's next generation of fours, the 1·6-litre GM and the 1,131 c.c. MY, delivered their brake horses at more modest rates of rotation.

41 CROSSLEY 25–30 h.p., 1919, Great Britain

Essentially 1914 in concept, the Crossley changed its image drastically between its introduction in 1910 and its disappearance from the range fifteen years later.

The first '20 h.p.' models designed by Hubert Woods were renowned for four-wheel brakes of uncoupled type—less satisfactory than Argyll's coupled system. Woods' fastest time of day at Coalport Hill-Climb in 1911 heralded a long line of similar successes, in which the smaller 15 h.p. 'Shelsley' sporting model shared. The front-wheel brakes were dropped after 1912, but by late 1914 'sporting' Crossleys wore the rounded-vee radiator, which the works (unofficially) termed a 'troutnose'. Meanwhile the model had been adopted by the youthful Royal Flying Corps, which had 80 on charge by January, 1914. The Royal Naval Air Service followed suit, the Commander-in-Chief, Aldershot, rode in a 25–30 landaulette, and the famous tenders with their canvas tilts and twin rear tyres were to be seen wherever British forces fought. Thanks to these Government orders production continued without a break in the 1914–18 period, and as early as February, 1919, the Gorton works were turning out cars to civilian account.

'Troutnose' radiators were now standard, but the electrics apart, the model had changed little. The indestructible engine boasted a five-bearing crankshaft and lubrication by pressure and splash, cooling was by thermosyphon with fan assistance, and the carburetter was a four-jet Smith. The frame had tubular cross-members, and the 25–30 rode on detachable wire wheels. Old-fashioned were the non-detachable head and foot transmission brake, but the big Crossley would do 55–60 m.p.h., even with ponderous formal coachwork which increased weight to around 2¼ tons. Prices were inflated: a tourer which cost £575 ($2,875) in 1914 now retailed at £1,375 ($6,875).

None the less, the 25–30 established the Crossley as correct proconsular wear. Among the clients were the Prince of Wales (who used the model on his 1921 Indian tour), and the King of Siam, while the Court-Treatts chose a brace of modified 25–30s for their Cape–London marathon in 1924–26.

42 LANCHESTER 40, 1919, Great Britain

George Lanchester's last pre-War design, the Sporting Forty, represented the triumph of commercialism over inspired thinking, in that the traditional Lanchester forward control had given way to an orthodox bonnet, while for the first and last time side valves had been seen on a car of this make. His 1919 Forty, while outwardly similar, was a great improvement. The cantilever rear suspension, silent worm drive, and three-speed epicyclic gearbox were inherited from earlier models, but under the bonnet was a new 12-valve six with aluminium crankcase and a single overhead camshaft driven by worm gearing from a vertical shaft at the front. There was dual ignition, and the full-pressure lubrication system was augmented by a second pump for the gearbox. Both the foot transmission brake and the rear-wheel hand-brake were of internal-expanding type. Buyers had the choice of two wheelbase lengths—141 and 150 inches. The chassis price (£1,800 in 1921) was set at £50 below Rolls-Royce's 'Silver Ghost'.

Unlike Rolls-Royce, Lanchester made their own bodies with cast light alloy framing and duralumin panels. Sub-frames of light steel and rubber mounts were also used, and a 40 h.p. tourer weighed about 3,960 pounds, giving a top speed of 78 m.p.h. Much heavier, of course, was the 1919 London Show car, an ornate four-seater saloon for the owner-driver with inlaid marquetry roof, of which King George V was heard to observe that it was 'more suited to a prostitute than a prince'.

The Forty did not acquire four-wheel brakes until 1924, when a combination of mechanical actuation and hydraulic servo assistance was adopted, soon supplanted by an all-mechanical Dewandre servo. The model remained current until 1929–30, about 500 being delivered. Among the customers were King George VI (when Duke of York), and such Indian potentates as the Maharajah of Alwar, who commissioned a fantastic state landau in which the passenger compartment rested upon cee-springs. A specially tuned version with lightweight single-seater bodywork took 24 World's Long-Distance Records at Brooklands, in August, 1924, covering 1,000 miles at 95·72 m.p.h.

43 PICCARD-PICTET
15CV, 1919, Switzerland

Switzerland's motor industry was facing a crisis in 1919. The wartime boom occasioned by four years without foreign imports was over, and the outside world demanded cheaper transportation than Martini or Piccard-Pictet could offer. Admittedly a protectionist policy ensured that Swiss citizens bought Swiss whenever possible; even in 1923, the Pic-Pic was the Confederacy's third most popular make, with 751 examples in circulation. There were, however, already 1,499 FIATs in use.

Piccard-Pictet succeeded the Société d'Automobiles à Genève, founded in 1904 to build Marc Birkigt's Hispano-Suizas under licence. This venture had folded four years later, but a new company was responsible for some interesting vehicles using a variant of Argyll's single-sleeve-valve engine, this being preferred to the Swiss Dufour design. A high point was reached in 1914 with the 4½-litre French Grand Prix cars, which boasted an alleged 150 b.h.p. at 3,000 r.p.m., wore handsome vee-radiators, and four-wheel brakes— another similarity with the Argyll, though the Swiss car's hydraulic shock absorbers were something the Scottish firm had not adopted.

The post-War models retained the Burt engine, in conjunction with dry-sump lubrication, twin oil pumps, tubular connecting-rods, and pump and fan cooling. The four-speed gearbox and multi-disc clutch were mounted in unit with the engine, and along with a 3-litre four there was a 6-litre vee-eight, on which coupled four-wheel brakes were standard, though the smaller 15CV retained the old rear-wheel and transmission arrangements. It was a heavy and expensive car on a 123-inch wheelbase, weighing 3,650 pounds, and a list price of £1,395 ($6,975) made it too expensive for Britons, even though it was nearly as quiet as the more popular Knight engine apart from 'slight gobbling sounds' at low revs.

Alas for Piccard-Pictet, their liabilities had piled up to 24 million Swiss francs, and the Ateliers de Charmilles, a firm of turbine manufacturers, had to mount a rescue operation. By 1921 the 15CV was back in small-scale production, and a year later some new finance was forthcoming. The *marque* struggled on a little longer, exhibiting at the 1924 Geneva Salon, but this was their swansong.

44 **APPERSON 8–20**, 1920, U.S.A.

'Where'd that Apperson come from—The Ark?' enquired the used-car dealer in John Steinbeck's *The Grapes of Wrath*, and by the depressed 1930s the *marque* was all but forgotten. But until 1926, Kokomo, Indiana, was a minor automobile centre, housing not only the Apperson Brothers' Automobile Company, but also Haynes, founded by the Appersons' erstwhile partner, with whom they had tested a prototype in July 1894. They parted company with Elwood Haynes in 1902, and for the next few years they concentrated on automobiles of some performance, made in limited numbers. The mon-strous Type-D speedster, rated at 95 b.h.p. retailed at $10,500 in 1906 and the subsequent Jackrabbits were also notable performers. In 1916, however, the company launched the first of their 90-degree vee-eights, publicised under the name of 'Roadaplane'. Capacity was just under four litres, and specification was entirely straightforward, with three-speed gearbox, spiral bevel final drive, and all brakes on the rear wheels. Capacity was up to 5·4 litres by 1918, when C. T. Silver, Apperson's New York dealer, promoted a range of elegant 'Silver' Appersons with sporting bodies renowned for the bevelled-edge treatment. These paved the way for some even more handsome creations on Kissel chassis in 1919.

By this time the vee radiator of the first Apperson eights had given way to something in the FIAT idiom, and the 8–20 was a satisfactory, if not a spectacular performer on 70 b.h.p.; 1920–21 models, which sold for $3,500 at home and for £1,150 in England, came on a 130-inch wheelbase.

Alas, a small maker could no longer subsist in the increasingly competitive U.S. market, and Apperson, who produced most of their car themselves, had never sold more than 2,000 units a year. A sign of decline was the use of bought-out proprietary engines—a Falls Six in 1923, and then the big Lycoming straight-eight favoured by their fellow-Indianians, Auburn. The 1925 Jackrabbit Straightaway Eight was an impressive-looking car, especially in fabric sports coupé form (an unusual departure for an American factory), but the 1926 models were the last.

45 BRIGGS AND STRATTON FLYER, 1920, U.S.A.

The Briggs and Stratton was probably the only five-wheeled passenger car to be sold in commercial quantities, but even by cyclecar standards it plumbed depths of barbarity hitherto unanticipated.

Surprisingly it had quite a long career, starting off as the Smith Flyer (by A. O. Smith of Milwaukee) in 1917, and ending as the electrically-propelled Auto Red Bug, albeit with a mere four wheels, in 1928. The chassis consisted of six wooden slats reinforced by wooden cross members, plus further reinforcement in channel steel at each end. This primitive structure rode upon cycle-type wire wheels with mudguards to match, the only other 'bodywork' being two wooden bucket seats upholstered (though only partly) in 'moroccoline leather'.

If anything, the mechanical elements were still cruder. There was an air-cooled single-cylinder auto-wheel unit complete with petrol tank, mounted centrally behind the rear axle, drive being engaged when it was lowered *via* a handle in front of the driver. Of gears and suspension there were none, and the footbrake was of block type, working on both rear tyres. Other controls were limited to a motorcycle-type throttle on the steering-wheel, and an exhaust valve lifter. Ignition was by flywheel magneto, and the cooling was fan-assisted. A disc on the driving wheel gave the engine better protection from road dust than the crew enjoyed.

This delightful *ensemble* weighed around 245 pounds, and factory pub-

licity claimed over 80 m.p.g. (which was optimistic) and 25 m.p.h., which was reasonably accurate. 'Just imagine riding,' said an advertisement, 'along some delightful boulevard or over a picturesque country road with a charming young lady for companion.' Unfortunately $335-worth of Ford did it both better and in far greater comfort, which is why the Flyer never became 'one of the most popular contrivances ever brought out for Young America'. The Auto Red Bug, however, enjoyed a vogue at French seaside resorts, where it appealed to those too chicken-hearted to brave the ocean on a *pedalo*.

46 ESSEX FOUR, 1920, 1921, U.S.A.

Hudson already had something of a performance-image with their Super Six, introduced in 1916. When they decided to bid for the cheap-car market with a four-cylinder companion model, they retained these virtues. For all its splash lubrication and angular style, the i.o.e. Essex was good for 60 m.p.h. in standard form, while abbreviated versions figured in the awards lists of the 1920, 1922, and 1923 Pikes Peak hill-climbs, and a stripped but otherwise stock model circled Cincinnati Speedway in appalling weather conditions for 48 hours, averaging 60·66 m.p.h. The British concessionaires campaigned the Essex energetically, with numerous sprint successes in the 1920–22 period: it actually beat a 3-litre Bentley at Holme Moss on one occasion, and lap speeds of more than 85 m.p.h. were attained at Brooklands. A number were used for rural mail deliveries in the United States.

Its valve gear and traditional wet-plate clutch apart, the Essex was a conventional automobile distinguished only by its rectangular radiator shell with horizontal shutters that actually worked, and were no mere styling gimmick. It sold well, accounting for more than half Hudson's 40,054 sales in 1919, and by 1923 the combined contribution of the two *marques* added up to close on 89,000 cars. 1922 saw the first of the ugly Essex coaches, uncompromisingly angular and with piano-type door hinges—they were the first American sedans to sell at anything like open-car prices, retailing for only $100 more than a touring car. Thenceforward Hudson sold more closed cars than soft-tops.

Unfortunately for the enthusiastic driver, 1924 saw the replacement of the Four by a new, small Essex Six. At 2·1 litres it was appreciably less powerful, though it was cheaper to make, and helped Hudson score their all-time sales record of 300,962 cars in 1929. But even at under $600, it was destined to be a casualty of the Depression, and though the first of Hudson's 1932 Terraplane models bore the Essex emblem, the *marque* became a 'lost cause' in 1933.

47 FORD MODEL-T, 1920, U.S.A.

By the end of World War I the Model-T was acquiring the status of an automobile coelocanth.

In 1908 a four-cylinder touring car capable of 40 m.p.h. was something of a sensation at $850 (£170), while such aids to servicing as detachable cylinder heads were virtually unknown. The two-speed, pedal-controlled planetary transmission was common American practice, also found on makes like Buick and Reo, while appalling roads and an unmechanically-minded population called for simplicity and toughness as well as a bargain price. The Ford filled the bill admirably. Aided by its creator's sophisticated manufacturing methods—a moving assembly line was installed in 1913—the Model-T had become the World's Universal Car. In less well-developed countries the boom reached vast proportions: in 1914 New South Wales alone registered 1,043 Fords, more than double the contribution of any other individual make. Britain's best-selling car was also the Ford, assembled in a factory at Trafford Park, Manchester, and selling at a low £125 in two-seater form.

In 1920 the picture was rather different. Three-speed sliding-type gearboxes were universal even on the cheapest cars, and firms of the calibre of Willys-Overland and Chevrolet were offering conventionally-controlled vehicles at near-Ford prices. If 'Lizzie's' rather rudimentary brakes were no worse than anyone else's, Henry Ford was the only major manufacturer in the U.S.A. not to standardise either electric starters or demountable rims—both were optional extras in 1920, and even in 1925 one could still buy a touring car with the infuriating magneto-driven headlamps (as the revs dropped in high gear, the illumination faded to a dull glow), hand-starting, and an oil tail-lamp.

But 'Lizzie' was exceedingly cheap— $315 for a touring car, and only $660

(£132) for a 'center-door' sedan in 1921—the 'Fordor' closed cars came later. She was just as fool-proof as ever, and parts could be bought off the counter almost anywhere. Hence production mounted: over a million in 1922, and a resounding 1,817,891 the following year, a season's performance that was not to be bettered (ironically, by Chevrolet) until 1955. It should also be remembered that for all today's mass production methods it took until 1972 for Volkswagen to surpass the total output of 'T's with their ubiquitous 'Beetle'.

48 DARRACQ TYPE-A
25CV, 1920, France

The product of a French factory within a British-controlled combine, the Darracq was going through an uneasy phase when nobody seemed quite sure what to call it. When Automobiles Darracq bought Clément-Talbot of London in October, 1919, the French cars became Talbot-Darracqs, but with the addition of Sunbeam to the consortium Frenchmen started to refer to the cars from Suresnes as plain 'Talbot', pronounced à la Française.

Alas, one of S.T.D.'s great failings was an infinite ability to compete against itself, and in the 4½-litre class they had three totally different offerings—the rapid 25–50 h.p. four-cylinder Talbot from London, Wolverhampton's big side-valve Sunbeam six (soon to acquire pushrod o.h.v.) and now Owen Clegg's French swansong, a side-valve vee-eight intended to repeat the success of Leland's 1915 Cadillac, and, incidentally, to continue

what de Dion-Bouton had started way back in 1910.

The big Darracq had a number of American features, among them coil ignition, central ball change for its four-speed unit gearbox, and all brakes on the rear wheels, though anchors on the front wheels had been added by the close of 1920. The cantilever rear suspension made sense on a big and heavy car—wheelbase was a lengthy 138 inches, and a tourer turned the scales at nearly 4,000 pounds. By American standards the 25CV had a respectable power-to-weight ratio, 80 b.h.p. being delivered at 2,600 r.p.m. Top speed was about 65 m.p.h.

But only Detroit can build American, and the Darracq remained a rather unhappy compromise. It was extremely flexible, pulling down to a walking pace on the 3·85 to 1 top gear, but it suffered from poor roadholding and a great thirst for fuel, while in England it cost very little less (at £1,450) than the well-tried Cadillac as promoted by the energetic Fred Bennett. Less than 500 were made, and though the model was still quoted in 1924 production had ceased some time previously. Darracq (or Talbot) went back to the excellent four-cylinder cars created by Owen Clegg in 1913, moving on to a family of equally solid pushrod sixes in 1926.

49 CARDEN 7–8 h.p., 1920,
Great Britain

Sir John Carden, who was killed in an airliner crash in 1935, was a prolific inventor whose interests embraced ultra-light aircraft and amphibious tanks. He also devoted much time to cyclecar designs.

His first effort appeared in 1913, and was a crude, unitary-construction affair fabricated from half-inch ash planks. Power came from a rear-mounted 481 c.c. single-cylinder J.A.P. engine driving the back axle by roller chain. One pushed off, motorcycle-style, since there were no gears or free-engine clutch. This evolved into an improved version with 4 h.p. twin engine and two-speed countershaft gear, which sold for £72 10s. The design was subsequently taken up by A.V. Motors, who marketed in from 1919 to 1924.

Carden was back in 1919 with new front- and rear-engined projects using the 8 h.p. twin J.A.P. unit, but a year later he went into production at Ascot with a true £100 car.

This time he mounted his 707 c.c. two-stroke twin engine horizontally at the rear, in unit with a two-speed gearbox and wet-plate clutch, the whole being mounted on a solid rear axle which it drove by spur gear. Springing was by coils all round, and the power unit could be detached from its retaining saddle-piece by undoing two nuts—unfortunately it sometimes detached itself. The dummy bonnet and radiator concealed only the crew's legs. On a weight of 400 pounds this £100 Carden proved capable of an unreliable 40 m.p.h. Though in February, 1921, the factory claimed to be making them at the rate of a hundred a week, production ceased in 1922.

Carden tried again in 1923 with a revised model, the New Carden. This had a Clyno-like dummy radiator in the nose, leaf springing (transverse at the front), and a magneto in place of the 1920 car's coil. An alternative version, the Sheret, used an amidships-mounted engine and chain drive, but weight was up to 675 pounds and few of either type found buyers. The cyclecar was well and truly dead.

50 **ROLLS-ROYCE 40–50 h.p. SILVER GHOST,** 1920, Great Britain

The aftermath of World War I saw a new generation of luxury cars—the overhead-camshaft sixes of Lanchester and Hispano-Suiza, and Isotta Fraschini's pushrod straight-eight. Packard had been building twelves in quantity since 1916. Yet the Rolls-Royce was still the same old side-valve bi-block six it had been in 1906.

Output of the post-War Silver Ghost engine was about 68 b.h.p., to Packard's 88, Lanchester's 100, and Hispano-Suiza's 135, all from units of smaller capacity. Henry Royce was not to adopt four-wheel brakes (of Hispano-Suiza servo type) until 1924. Straight-line performance, however, mattered little in the carriage trade: Royce had always aimed at smoothness and flexibility, and his cars still met these criteria. A Ghost would pull away smoothly from a walking pace to 70 m.p.h. in top gear, and it was also more frugal than the opposition, being capable of a modest 16 m.p.g. As for those much-vaunted anchors on the front wheels, it is significant that Lanchester fitted them first to his 'small' 21 h.p. car, since it was felt that they were superfluous on the big Forty: really large cars were meant to be driven with circumspection. In any case, Royce had abandoned the transmission brake in 1913, and subsequent Ghosts had an effective system with both sets working in separate drums on the rear wheels. The *marque's* continuing *réclame* is reflected in the prices paid for good 1914 models in 1920–21; £7,000 ($35,000) was par for an Alpine Eagle tourer.

Post-War improvements were on a modest scale: alloy pistons and electric starters were standardised in 1919, and a subsidiary starting carburetter was added in 1921. The last Ghosts had spiral bevel gears in their rear axles, as well as four-wheel brakes.

Sales remained steady. When the line was discontinued in 1925, 6,173 had been made, while American production between 1921 and 1926 accounted for another 1,703, even if Americans preferred their Rolls-Royces 'fully imported'. After all, the Best Car in The World did look a trifle incongruous with the left-hand driving, three-speed gearbox and central change of Springfield's final Ghosts.

51 AGA 4/20 PS, 1920, Germany

After the Armistice the German motor industry was beset with a mulitplicity of problems. Inflation at home reduced the demand for cars to miserable proportions; even in 1925 there was only one car to every 316 Germans, as against 1 to 70 in France. Petrol and rubber were in short supply, and widespread anti-German feeling excluded Germany's cars from many markets. The end-product did not help the situation, for all too often it was ugly, with a vee-radiator, angular wings, and curiously nautical tail-end treatment. Despite the establishment of several consortia, there was little impetus for technical development, and many a firm kept going on conservative restatements of 1912–14 themes.

The Berlin-built Aga was a new make introduced in 1919, and it was inspired by the F.N. 1250 of 1914. The straightforward side-valve four-cylinder engine boasted pressure lubrication and a three-bearing crankshaft; output was 20–22 b.h.p. Unusual on so small a car were the 12-volt electrics and fuel feed by Autovac from a rear tank, and a three-speed unit gearbox featured in the specification. Wheelbase was 100 inches; a sporting version was also made, though this should not be confused with the special o.h.c. Agas which competed in the 1924 Targa Florio. The car was competitively priced, at 7,650 marks (about £380), and in 1922 the factory was talking of 1,000 4/20s a month. At the same time the model was being made under licence in Sweden as the Thulin.

This prosperity undoubtedly stemmed from Aga's membership of the industrial group headed by Hugo Stinnes (other members were Rabag, Bugatti's German licencee, and Dinos), but when Stinnes died in 1926, the firm collapsed, though not before they had added four-wheel brakes to the specification in 1925, as well as experimenting with a 'pneumatic' system which probably got no further than the Berlin Show.

Aga were reorganised, and deliveries of the s.v. fours continued until 1928.

The last new model was, however, of foreign origin—a version of the British 848 c.c. o.h.c. Singer Junior made under licence.

52 ANSALDO 4C, 1920, Italy

Ansaldo of Turin were one of Italy's biggest engineering firms, with a history dating back to pre-Risorgimento days. After the Armistice they found themselves burdened with surplus floor-space, and Ing. Soria, the head of their aero-engine division, was entrusted with the task of designing a touring car. The prototype was on the road by August 1919, and deliveries began the following year.

As befitted so large an organisation, they sought to challenge FIAT's national domination of the cheap-car market, and certainly the 4C was a simple and rather crude-looking automobile. In the best Italian tradition, most of the money had gone into the beautifully neat single o.h.c. four-cylinder engine with its detachable head, magneto ignition, and pump-and-fan circulation. The rest was fringe Detroit; a single dry plate clutch, wide-ratio three-speed unit gearbox, central ball change, open propeller shaft, and spiral bevel back axle (some early cars had plain bevels). The handbrake worked on the transmission and the standard body was an austere tourer, its resemblance to a Chevrolet accentuated by the plain radiator shell and artillery wheels. On a 4·6 to 1 top gear it was capable of about 50 m.p.h., though by 1923 more discriminating buyers could opt for the 4CS with wire wheels, and a 2-litre engine which developed 48 b.h.p. to the 4C's 35. This was a 70 m.p.h. motorcar.

The promised mass production never eventuated, and one may doubt if Ansaldo ever made more than two thousand cars in a single year. 1923 saw the company's first six, the 2-litre 6C, and in 1929 there was a 3½-litre straight-eight for the carriage trade. Soria, however, resigned in 1927, and with his departure all serious development ceased. When the firm got into difficulties in 1931, they sold their stock of unfinished cars to the O.M.-backed C.E.V.A. concern, and until 1936 it was still possible to buy a 'remaindered' Ansaldo of 1930 type with slightly revamped bodywork.

53 MARTINI TF, 1920, Switzerland

Of Switzerland's two leading producers in 1919, Martini were the stronger, having been making cars in series since 1902, though not without vicissitudes. Their versions of the French Rochet-Schneider were excellent cars, but in 1904 the company had come under the control of a Briton, H. H. P. Deasy. When Deasy left to make cars under his own name in Coventry another British group took over: when this concern, Hills-Martini Ltd., failed in 1908 there was a reversion to Swiss ownership. Soon afterwards a bank failure led to yet another reorganisation, but though this meant the abandonment of Martini's promising little o.h.c. *voiturette*, technical interest was by no means lacking. In 1913–14 there were a 25–35 h.p. sleeve-valve and a potent 16-valve o.h.c. 15 *Sport* with hemispherical combustion chambers. Already in 1911 13 per cent of all cars registered in Switzerland were Martinis, and the wartime car shortage led to a brief boom culminating in 1917, when the factory delivered 325 cars.

Their post-War TF was, however, a typical 1914 luxury tourer brought up to date with full electrics and detachable wheels. The big four-cylinder side-valve engine had a non-detachable head, fuel feed was by air pressure, and the footbrake worked on the transmission. There was a three-bearing crankshaft and a generously-dimensioned vee-radiator, while the Martini rifle emblem was also stamped on the inspection cover of the four-speed gearbox.

This sort of thing, naturally, was no longer competitive in export markets, where even the conservative customer had the choice of many a cheaper French model. Britons, of course, had the well-established 25–30 h.p. Crossley, and even when promoted by the energetic Rootes brothers the TF stood no chance against Manchester's finest on its native heath. The inevitable happened—there was another bankruptcy in 1920.

Martini struggled gamely on. Walter Steiger, a Swiss who had done quite well with his own sporting models in Germany, injected some further capital, and launched a family of side-valve sixes, culminating in the 4·4-litre NF-type of 1931, while alongside these latter-day creations Martini made (or more probably assembled) German Wanderers. Neither line prospered, and the last of Switzerland's great names was dead by 1934.

54 BERLIET VL, 16CV, 1921, France

Invariably a war breeds a huge demand for cars, and manufacturers are lulled into tempting one-model policies which lower production costs. Of such a stamp was the Standard Vanguard of 1948.

It is surprising, however, to find such an old hand as Marius Berliet falling for this particular chimera. His 1914 range of high-grade vehicles with s.v. monobloc four-cylinder engines extended from a modest 12CV up to the vast 6·3-litre Type-U, and thanks to a useful truck business he was making around 4,000 vehicles a year. He also had an excellent foothold in such markets as Argentina and Brazil.

His 1919 programme was, however, confined to one lorry, the indestructible 5-ton CBA, and a single passenger-car model, the 15CV VB-type. French writers summarised this as *une fausse Dodge*, which is exactly what it was, with a 3·3-litre side-valve four-cylinder engine, pump-and-trough lubrication, a three-speed unit gearbox with central ball change, and 12-volt electrics. There was Buick-type cantilever rear suspension, and a final American touch was the use of fixed disc wheels and detachable rims. The rounded radiator shell was pure Dodge, and Berliet's plan was to churn these crypto-Americans out at the rate of a hundred a day, thereby underwriting a list price of only 9,500 francs, or only 1,550 more than were asked for the contemporary 10CV Citroën, also a mass-produced vehicle.

The Citroën succeeded: the Berliet-Dodge backfired. Production stuck at fifteen a day, while American volume was not matched by American manufacturing techniques. Over 400 back axles had to be replaced under guarantee, so that the firm lost money on every car. Nor were the trucks exactly an insurance policy. True, they gave no trouble and could be made in adequate quantities, but they were competing against war-surplus vehicles at bargain-basement prices, and the double disaster forced Berkliet into receivership during 1921.

The VL was a rescue operation, and as such it was fairly successful. In essence it differed little from the crypto-Dodge, but a new and more Gallic radiator and bonnet line made all the difference, and though demountable rims were still standard, buyers had the option of wire wheels. Price was up to a more realistic 19,900 francs, and sales were adequate, even if the vehicle scarcely deserved its glamorous name of *Etoile d'Argent*. As late as 1934 Berliet were still making really large fours, that year's catalogue containing a 3·3-litre VRD rated at 19CV.

55 DE DION-BOUTON
10CV, 1921, France

One sad characteristic of French industry in the 1920s was the decline of many an old firm which had over-extended itself during the War, and now had nothing new to say. While such newcomers as Bugatti, Citroën, and Mathis forged ahead, and Renault made conservatism pay, De Dion-Bouton went quietly downhill. Their brilliant 1899 single-cylinder *voiturette* had been their mainstay for a decade, and if the smaller models which succeeded it were less inspired, there was evidence of progressive thought in the family of controversial vee-eights launched in 1910.

By 1921, however, convention was in command. Gone were the de Dion back axle and the famous decelerator pedal. The IC- and ID-types were good, average specimens of uprated 1914 design. Pre-War influences were detectable in the fixed cylinder head, the gear-driven camshaft, and the foot transmission brake, while modern ideas extended to a four-speed unit gearbox, alloy pistons and Michelin disc detachable wheels. The vee-radiator was not unattractive, and by this time de Dion made their own magnetos and electrical equipment under the Victrix brand-name, a legacy of the war years, when the Allies were suddenly cut off from the useful Herr Bosch. The 10CV was reliable, if undramatic, and owners spoke of fuel consumptions in the region of 33 m.p.g. The leisured gait of 45 m.p.h. mattered little to de Dion's clientele.

Unfortunately De Dion-Bouton fell between two stools—while abandoning the luxury market when the vee-eights were discontinued at the end of 1923, they failed to re-establish themselves in the runabout field in which they had made their name, quite simply because they lacked the resources to compete against Citroën, Renault, or Peugeot. 3,000 cars a year was very big business in 1905, but twenty years later aspirants for the big league had to think in terms of 20,000. 1923 four-cylinder de Dions were available with four-wheel brakes, overhead valves, and detachable heads, but they sold at upper-middle-class prices, and the company's cheap light car, the 1·3-litre JP-type, came too late in 1926.

56 VOISIN C4, 1921, 1923, France

That rugged individualist Gabriel Voisin is indelibly associated with *grand'routiers*, from his classic 4-litre 18CV of 1919 to the formidable straight-twelve that marked his effective swansong in 1937. At the 1921 Paris Salon, however, he launched a small luxury car, created from scratch in a mere five months.

The C4 was really a miniature 18CV, with monobloc four-cylinder Knight sleeve-valve engine, horizontal Zenith carburetter fed by gravity from a tank on the dash, cone clutch, three-speed unit box, central change, and semi-elliptic springs assisted by friction dampers. The 1,244 c.c. unit developed a respectable 26 b.h.p. at 3,000 r.p.m., propelling the little Voisin at 50–55 m.p.h., though it was expensive—£825 ($4,125) in England. As usual, the bodies reflected Voisin's heterodox thought, with piano-hinged doors, large luggage containers on the running-boards, and boxy closed styles covered in grey tartan fabric; though in later years most fours came with the more attractive *Lumineuse* style, a two-door victoria with rear trunk and excellent all-round vision. Front-wheel brakes became available in 1923, and power was steadily increased; 30 b.h.p. from 1,328 c.c. in 1924, and 44 b.h.p. at a high 4,400 r.p.m. in the final, 1,552 c.c. C7 series of 1925. This, the last of

the four-cylinder Voisins, persisted until 1928, with Dewandre servo brakes, top speed in closed two-seater form being quoted as 70 m.p.h

C4s were raced, an example winning its class in the 1923 *Circuit des Routes Pavées* over the appalling roads of Northern France, and the mechanical elements were used in the two-seater version of Voisin's extraordinary open *Laboratoire* models introduced in 1925. The C7 also nearly became one of the first cars to be marketed with an automatic transmission. It was successfully tested with the de Lavaud infinitely variable gear, but this disappeared suddenly after attractive rave notices in the press. Rumour said that a de Lavaud-equipped Citroën had disgraced itself while André's wife was at the wheel, and when Citroën cancelled his order any chances of marketing the device economically vanished.

57 LEYLAND EIGHT, 1921, 1923, Great Britain

J. G. Parry Thomas's contender for the luxury stakes was unveiled in 1920, initially with a capacity of 6,967 c.c., increased on production cars to 7·3 litres. One of the first straight-eights to reach the market, it featured a detachable head, a single overhead camshaft with drive by triple eccentrics, inclined valves, and hemispherical combustion chambers. The crankshaft ran in six main bearings, and full-pressure lubrication was used: ignition was by coil. The output was 110 b.h.p. at 2,200 r.p.m., with a maximum potential of 145 b.h.p. The four-speed box and single-plate clutch were conventional, but the starter motor was incorporated in the gearbox, and actuated by movement of the lever.

The chassis was equally advanced. The quarter-elliptic rear springs incorporated a torsion bar, and were also made to operate plungers for an automatic lubrication system. Though there were brakes only on the rear wheels, these were given vacuum servo assistance, with mechanical actuation available in the event of a servo failure. Maintenance was also considered: there were two steering boxes, so that the column itself did not intrude into the engine compartment. Buyers had the choice of three wheelbase lengths, and inevitably the Leyland was very expensive: £1,875 ($9,375) for a chassis, and £2,700 ($13,500) for a touring car.

Only about fourteen were made. One went to Michael Collins in Dublin, while another two were shipped to the Maharajah of Patiala in India: as Leyland issued no instruction manual, Reid Railton, Thomas's assistant, was sent out with the cars to instruct His Highness's Motor Superintendent in their ways.

In fact the Leyland's fame stemmed from Thomas's exploits with the cars at Brooklands, a programme of which the factory did not approve, and which eventually led to a parting of the ways. With four Zenith carburetters the big engine was persuaded to give 200 b.h.p., and the lightweight Leyland–Thomas recorded 129·74 m.p.h. at the Track.

Leyland, like Berliet, suffered from the glut of ex-service commercial vehicles, and their problems were not helped by their own insistence on buying up huge numbers of these trucks

and reconditioning them themselves. The Leyland Eight was abandoned in 1923; thereafter the firm's sole passenger-car offering was the austere two-stroke Trojan, made in their branch works at Kingston-upon-Thames.

58 **STAR 11·9 h.p.**, 1921–22, Great Britain

The English equivalent of firms like Apperson was Star of Wolverhampton, who had been building cars since 1898, and were still manufacturing at the rate of twenty units a week in the early 1920s, this despite cramped premises situated in a warren of back streets. They were self-contained, with their own foundry and body shops, and the astronomical theme was pursued in the names they gave to their coachwork ('Libra', 'Jason', 'Scorpio').

The 11·9 h.p. introduced in mid-1921 was a copybook middle-class family tourer conceived with an eye on the horsepower tax: side valves, detachable cylinder head, magneto ignition, splash lubrication, three-speed unit gearbox, rear-wheel brakes, and spiral bevel back axle. Star preferred a single dry plate clutch to the established cone, and unusual in a 'class' car were the central change and the disc wheels, though steel artilleries were provided on the costlier 'Special' variants, which retailed for about £50 more. The 1,795 c.c. engine developed 27 b.h.p. at 2,000 r.p.m., which was sufficient to propel a 2,128-pound automobile at 50 m.p.h. It was, of course, a light car only by Star's standards, with a wheelbase of 108 inches. 'Dipping headlights' were featured in the specification, but in fact application of the dipswitch merely extinguished the headlamps, leaving the driver to manage as best he could on the sidelamps!

In 1923 capacity was increased to 1,945 c.c., and the range included a coachbuilt sedan at £725 ($3,625), while in 1925 there was a further addition to the shape of an o.h.v. 12–40, capable of 70 m.p.h. and sold only in two-seater form. This one came with four-wheel brakes, these being an optional extra on 1926 models of the basic 12–25. By 1927 the only side-valve four-cylinder Star was the bigger 14–30, and after 1929 there were no fours at all. Star, now controlled by the Guy truck firm, moved to a larger factory at Bushbury, outside Wolverhampton, where they continued to manufacture attractive and well-appointed sixes until 1932. Latterly the resemblance to their fellow-Wulfrunians, the Sunbeams, became more pronounced, but neither make could keep its head above water on limited outputs and prices in the £500–£1,000 bracket.

59 RUMPLER OA 104, 1921, Germany

In the early 1920s the spiritual homes of convention were Britain (where resistance to change is endemic) and Germany (still dogged by inflation and internal unrest). A new generation of advanced light-alloy power units and sophisticated suspensions had yet to transform Berlin into the most exciting motor show of the European calendar.

Thus Edmund Rumpler's 1921 *tropfenwagen* (tear-drop car) was something

of a bombshell, though he had already designed and tested a swing-axle suspension for Adler as long ago as 1904. What is more, the extraordinary vehicle was actually made and sold in small numbers.

The basis of the Rumpler was a light steel hull of boat or aeroplane-fuselage shape with pressed-steel bulkheads in lieu of orthodox cross-members, and openings for springs and axles. The front suspension was conventional, but there was an independent swing-axle arrangement at the rear: all springs were mounted inboard. The engine and transmission unit was at the rear, an extension of the gearbox main shaft driving the wheels directly. Passenger accommodation was aeronautical: the driver sat in solitary state in the nose with not even a vestigial hood to spoil his view, while the passengers were located amidships to assure the maximum comfort. Nothing was allowed to upset the streamline shape: the headlamps were faired into the nose, the sidelamps lived on the tiny pontoon-shaped front wings, and the spare wheels were stored horizontally in hatches in the side of the body. Even the motor was unusual, being a water-cooled W-formation six on aircraft lines made for Rumpler by Siemens. It was rated at a modest 36 b.h.p., but good aerodynamics enabled the heavy (2,975 pounds) car to attain 70 m.p.h. Later versions used a 2·6-litre four-cylinder in-line o.h.v. unit of Rumpler's own make, which developed 50 b.h.p., and speed went up to over 80 m.p.h. Front-wheel brakes were standardised in 1925.

Though Benz used Rumpler's ideas for their 1924 2-litre Grand Prix car,

Rumpler himself turned to the exploration of front-wheel drive, and the last car to bear his name was the Ru6A-104, an open tourer of relatively conventional appearance powered by his four-cylinder 10/50 PS engine.

60 MOTO-COR, 1921, Italy

The cyclecar boom of 1912–22 passed Italy by, and most of her numerous miniatures date from the troubled and petrol-starved 1940s and 1950s. In any case there was no market for any kind of people's car in the last chaotic days before Mussolini's March on Rome: FIAT deemed it advisable to shelve their promising baby car, the *Modello-500*, which was on test in 1918.

One who swam against the tide was Armino Mezzo of Turin, and his odd little Moto-Cor was announced in 1921. Mechanically it drew on motor-cycle practice, the 'power pack' being a large motorbike minus its front fork, these elements being easily detachable by lifting the body and sliding them out. Buyers had the choice of two s.v. flat-twin air-cooled engines (said to be of British manufacture): their respective capacities were 575 c.c. and 745 c.c., and the bigger one could be had with pushrod o.h.v. as well. Lubrication was by drip feeds, and lighting was by acetylene, though the three-speed gearbox incorporated a reverse.

The body wore a dummy radiator in the bows, and all Moto-Cors had tandem seating, the driver sitting in the front, except on taxi versions, where he occupied the rear seat. There was also a parcelcar variant. On a weight of 445 pounds, Mezzo claimed a top speed of about 40 m.p.h., but though the Moto-Cor survived for two years, precious few were sold—probably not more than fifty.

In 1924 Mezzo tried again with a more conventional four-wheeler lightweight which he called the Edit. This was powered by a 1-litre vertical-twin engine and had a three-speed-and-reverse gearbox, but though it was advertised in the Italian motoring press, it did not progress beyond the prototype stage.

61 MINERVA 30CV, 1921, Belgium

Sylvain de Jong started a bicycle factory at Antwerp in 1897, branching out into a successful line of proprietary motor-cycle engines before undertaking the manufacture of complete vehicles. His first luxury car was the excellent six-cylinder 40 of 1907, but two years later Minerva adopted the Knight double-sleeve-valve engine and concentrated their efforts on fours. These were excellent performers, distinguishing themselves in the Austrian Alpine Trials and the tough Swedish Winter event, which their Stockholm concessionaire Hans Osterman won outright in 1911, 1913 and 1914.

The firm recovered rapidly from the German occupation, and cars were being delivered again by the end of 1919, albeit initially they made only a 20CV four. The parallel six did not appear in any quantity until 1921.

This model marked the beginning of Minerva's chauffeur-driven image which was to persist until the end in 1938, and closely paralleled the career of

France's Delaunay-Belleville in pre-1914 days. It was a large car on a 143-inch wheel-base, with cantilever rear suspension, and the cylinders of the sleeve-valve engine were cast monobloc: the massive seven-bearing crankshaft was lubricated on the traditional trough-and-dipper system. In its original guise the car had a fabric-faced cone clutch and a foot transmission brake, but early improvements included an easier single-plate clutch and pedal-operated rear-wheel brakes, replaced by servo-assisted anchors on all four wheels by 1923.

For all its magnificent under-bonnet finish, the 30 was not for the owner driver. Even with fairly simple body-work it turned the scales at two-and-a-half tons, and all the controls were immensely heavy. Not that it was a sluggard: top speed was 70–75 m.p.h., and a good example would put 38–40 miles into the hour without undue difficulty. By 1927 it had evolved into the faster and even heavier 5,954 c.c. AK-type, also made in short-chassis sporting form. Though straight-eights were made from 1929–30, the very large sixes were still available on paper as late as 1936.

62 SPYKER 30–40 h.p., 1921, The Netherlands

The only Dutch *marque* to acquire an international reputation before the advent of the ingenious belt-driven D.A.F. in 1958, the Spyker had been renowned in pre-1914 days for its round radiator, some interesting experiments with four-wheel drive, and a curious transverse-camshaft engine

produced in the 1909–16 period. After a brief skirmish with an uninspired and underpowered 13–30 h.p. side-valve four, the company turned in 1920 to a big luxury machine adorned with a handsome rounded-vee radiator in the N.A.G. or Delaunay-Belleville idiom.

The chassis was a massive affair with semi-elliptic suspension, and power was transmitted by a four-speed gearbox. Spyker, however, could no longer afford their own engines, and the 72 b.h.p. side-valve six came from Maybach of Germany, being fitted in that firm's ingenious W2 model. Head and block were integral, there was dual ignition with two plugs per cylinder, and the cooling fan incorporated a three-speed gear. Maybach's patent 'flameproof' carburetter was mounted low down and integral with the block, while other interesting features of the 30–40 included a curious M-shaped gear gate, a cast aluminium dash, and a serrated bar on the luggage grid, said to prevent small boys from hitching unauthorised rides. An early example was submitted to an official 30,000-mile trial, whence it emerged with flying colours, though thirteen valve springs had to be replaced. Despite a high weight (4,816 pounds with open tourer body) the Spyker was capable of 70 m.p.h., and fuel consumption was a reasonable 13 m.p.g.

Not that this car had much future in the contracting luxury market. S. F. Edge chose a Spyker in 1922 to attack his Double-Twelve Hour Record (taken in 1907 with a Napier) at Brooklands, and turned in a very consistent performance to average 74·27 m.p.h. Queen Wilhelmina herself ordered a brace of 30–40 h.p.

landaulettes, one of which was still running when the Germans occupied the Netherlands in 1940, but statistics tell their own story. Spyker bought 225 engines from Maybach, but were able to use only 150 of these. 1924 saw the necessary addition of four-wheel brakes, but the Spyker was too expensive for the home market, and lacked sufficient *cachet* to sell abroad. The Trompanburg factory closed in 1925.

63 DUESENBERG MODEL-A, 1922, U.S.A.

Fred S. Duesenberg was already renowned as a racing-car and engine designer when he made his first straight-eight in 1919: his 'walking-beam' four-cylinder proprietary unit powered many an American sports car of the period, notably the Roamer and the Biddle. He was racing eights by 1920, and towards the end of the year he launched a passenger car which stood head and shoulders above the standard American offering. Well it might, for prices ran around the $6,000 (£1,200) mark.

Heart of his Model-A was a three-bearing overhead-camshaft unit of 4·3 litres capacity, developing 90 b.h.p. at 3,600 r.p.m.; an average American 4-litre engine, the Nash, disposed of a mere 55 b.h.p., and even the sophisticated o.h.c. Wills-Sainte Claire vee-eight, which was bigger than the Duesenberg, claimed only 67 brake horses. The camshaft drive was by vertical shaft, and there was full-pressure lubrication by gear-type pump. Aluminium pistons were standard, though conservative customers could

specify cast-iron ones; on later As the Stewart vacuum feed gave way to an Autopulse electric pump. If the chassis was conventional apart from its five cross-members, the hydraulically-actuated four-wheel brakes working in 16-inch drums were revolutionary by any standards. All Duesenbergs rode on Rudge-Whitworth quick-detachable wire wheels.

The cars distinguished themselves in long-distance endurance tests, notably a 3,155-mile observed run at Indianapolis Speedway at an average of 62·63 m.p.h. Top speed in standard form was around 80 m.p.h., but Duensenberg Specials evolved under the 1930 'Junk Formula' went away very fast at Indianapolis, Ira Hall finishing 8th at 98·21 m.p.h. in 1932.

Not many As were made—probably around 600 between 1921 and 1926, and many of these wore uninspired bodywork, though at least one speedster in the Auburn idiom saw the light of day. After E. L. Cord's purchase of Duesenberg, a handful of cars were delivered in 1927 and 1929 under the Model-X designation.

Under Cord's direction, of course, Fred Duesenberg produced his masterpiece, the fantastic, 6·9-litre 265 b.h.p. twin o.h.c. Model-J of 1929, destined to be one of the great cars of all time. It stands to Duesenberg's credit that the company was able to sell 470 of these monsters between then and 1937.

64 TEMPLAR, 1922, U.S.A.

Not all the more individual American cars were elephantine. For most of its life the Cleveland-built Templar combined a 3·2-litre four-cylinder engine with a modest wheelbase of 118 inches, and the firm contrived to sell about 7,500 cars between 1917 and 1924, even if annual production never exceeded 1,700 units, in their best year of 1920.

The car was modelled outwardly on Erik Delling's handsome and rapid 22–70 h.p. L-head Mercer: radiators were similar in shape, and Templar's 'Sportette', a four-seater tourer, closely resembled the 'Sporting' Mercer. In one respect, indeed, the Templar was more advanced, for its engine boasted pushrod o.h.v., something which Mercer did not adopt until their disastrous Rochester-engined six. Templar units developed 43 b.h.p. at 2,100 r.p.m., and featured three-bearing balanced crankshafts, full-pressure lubrication, ignition by magneto, and vacuum feed. The three-speed gearbox, dry-plate clutch, six-volt electrics and spiral bevel final drive were accepted American practice, and all brakes were of internal-expanding type. The more sedate models wore wooden wheels, but 'Sportette' and 'Roadster' variants came with six wire wheels; on the latter the buyer also got a compass, a Kodak camera, and 'hand pads' on the doors embossed with the Templar Cross. Britons who encountered their first (and probably their last) Templars in 1920 were also intrigued to find a 'hand choke' and an ignition key on the dash.

The fours from Cleveland were, admittedly, cheaper than any Mercer, but they were still too expensive, and post-War inflation took its toll of the modest sales. Price rose, from $2,185 (£437) in 1918 to $2,885 (£577) in 1921. Too late the company slashed its prices in 1922, but the only consequences were a receivership and a change of policy. The last Templars were very ordinary, if good-looking side-valve 4·4-litre sixes, and even their four-wheel brakes could not save the day.

65 WILLS-SAINTE CLAIRE, 1922, U.S.A.

Childe Harold Wills was a brilliant metallurgist and engineer, who parted company with his old employer, Henry Ford, in 1919, and used his one-and-a half million dollar golden handshake to finance not only a car bearing his name, but also a model industrial community at Marysville, Michigan.

The result was both handsome and sophisticated. Wills's wartime aero-engine experience was reflected in his choice of the vee-eight Hispano-Suiza motor as his exemplar. Like Birkigt, Wills favoured one overhead camshaft per block with spiral bevel gear drive, while block and head construction closely followed Hispano practice. Connecting-rods were of fork-blade type, there was a clutched fan, and the dual-choke Zenith carburetter lived in the angle between the blocks. The American designer, however, preferred cast iron for his cylinder blocks where the French (though not the Spanish) Hispano engines had used alloy. The dry multi-disc clutch was superior to the cone of early H6 Hispanos, while the Wills chassis followed orthodox American practice. The elegant radiator was undeniably inspired by the French car, as was the 'Gray Goose' mascot—as close as Wills could get to the *cigogne volante* without blatant plagiarism. Screenwipers and a reversing light were standard equipment at the factory price of $3,000 (£600).

Unfortunately the Wills was too complicated for the American market. The engines were expensive to buy and also to service, and sales were not encouraging, with a sharp drop from 4,300 in 1922 to 1,500 in 1923. Single-disc clutches and hydraulic four-wheel brakes were added in 1924, and though the vee-eight was still offered in 1925, it was replaced with a six thereafter.

This was a simpler car—the detachable cylinder head made for easier servicing. It was also just as advanced, with electric pump feed and the hydraulic brakes of the superseded model. Unfortunately it was also heavier (if only by about fifteen pounds), and the company went to the wall in 1927.

66 CYCLAUTO, 1922,
France

In France the cyclecar had a longer vogue than in other countries, if only because it possessed a legal status, albeit a slightly odd one. The regulations stipulated a capacity of not more than 1,100 c.c., seats for no more than two (which at least spared Frenchmen some of the perilous 'occasional-threes' fashionable on the other side of the Channel), and a maximum weight of 350 kilograms.

These standards could be met only by the lightest and simplest three-wheelers, such as Darmont's version of the British Morgan. Almost everyone else sat firmly on the wrong side of the fiscal abyss, whence not even such unacceptable economies as acetylene lamps could rescue them; ergo, these unfortunates circumvented the law by

selling their cars with two invoices, a 'stripped' one for the tax-man, and a second piece of paper listing all the forbidden extras. Understandably the Government gave up the unequal struggle after 1925, and one may wonder whether the later, four-cylinder Cyclautos did in fact conform to the definition.

The marque certainly did in 1919, when an original 1912 theme was revived with an ingenious space-frame of great rigidity, terminating in the fork which held the single front wheel. Power was provided by a 496 c.c. vertical-twin two-stroke engine which drove the rear wheels by belt. The two-speed planetary gear dispensed with a reverse, and there was the curious combination of pedal-controlled change and a lever for the selection of neutral. The vehicle was said to weigh 440 pounds, but by 1922 this version had given way to something far more car-like, with shaft drive, orthodox transmission, and a small o.h.v. four-cylinder C.I.M.E. engine, said to deliver 25 b.h.p. and to propel the Cyclauto at rates far beyond the 40 m.p.h. of the old twin. It was also a two-seater, whereas the 1919 model had been a monocar. The front fork was now faired into the short hood, and the price was a mere 9,500 francs.

67 HOTCHKISS AL, 1922,
France

Le juste milieu was Hotchkiss's slogan, and by 1922 that milieu was drifting away from such enormous sixes as the 9½-litre V-type of 1906. Gone also was the round radiator, replaced by a handsome horseshoe which inevitably attracted comparisons with the Bugatti. The crossed guns on the badge still reminded customers that Benjamin Berkeley Hotchkiss had been making cannon for Napoleon III in the Franco-Prussian War, while post-War financial stringency was reflected in the use of conventional torque-tube drive, and this on a make which had given its name to a method of drive *via* the springs.

The AL was the French equivalent of the Italian Lancia Theta and Kappa models, though its 132-inch wheelbase and weight, in open tourer form, of 4,060 pounds made it comparable also with the 25–30 h.p. Crossley. It was descended directly from the side-valve AF-type which Harry Ainsworth had driven in the 1914 Austrian Alpine Trial. This reappeared after the Armistice as the AH, still with foot transmission brake, cone clutch and separate four-speed gearbox, though now with full-pressure lubrication and an electric starter. Dynamo lighting, incidentally, had been listed before the War. 450 of these were sold in 1919 and 1920, but for 1921 the traditional Hotchkiss drive was scrapped, and cantilever springs used at the rear. Like Lancia, Hotchkiss switched to overhead valves and a detachable head in 1922, though on a modest 60 b.h.p. 55 m.p.h. was about the limit. Front-wheel brakes were added in 1923.

Once again, however, a change of *milieu* was indicated. Ainsworth, who had been managing Hotchkiss's Coventry works, fell out with his new master, W. R. Morris, and returned to France, where he master-minded a new one-model policy based on a modern 12CV with four-wheel brakes and (once

more) Hotchkiss drive. With a list price of less than 40,000 francs this one gave its makers a new lease of life. Annual sales climbed to over the thousand mark, and saved the company from the fate in store for de Dion-Bouton, Vermorel, and many others.

68 RENAULT 6CV, 1922, 1923, France

Louis Renault had made his name on small, cheap cars. His shaft-driven *voiturettes* with de Dion engines had led to the immortal twin-cylinder 1,100 c.c. AX of 1905–6, but in the immediate post-War period he had nothing smaller to offer than a solid 2·1-litre 10CV, which was hardly competition for the mass-produced A-type Citroën, let alone for that company's 5CV unveiled at the beginning of 1921. Even Mathis's SB was making some inroads.

The 6CV KJ of 1922 was his answer. In appearance it was traditional Renault, with its dashboard radiator standing proud of the coal-scuttle hood that had distinguished the *marque* since 1904. The four cylinders were cast monobloc, with thermo-syphon cooling and a detachable head, and Renault retained a magneto where Citroën preferred a coil. The transverse rear suspension, separate three-speed box and silent dynamotor starting were accepted Renault practice, but a central ball change was utilised. It was heavier than the Citroën at 1,512 pounds, but also faster, being capable of 45 m.p.h. to the Citroën's 38. In original guise it was at best a three-seater, though by 1924 four-seater bodywork was offered on a lengthened, 104-inch wheelbase. During its first season the appearance was improved by lowering the radiator to give a flush hood line, and cable-operated front-wheel brakes were standardised in 1925.

The price was competitive—17,450 francs in 1926, when it bridged the gap between the little Citroën at 14,375 fr., and its bigger sister, the 10CV, at 22,230 fr. Production was continued until 1929, deliveries working up to around a hundred a day at peak. The 6CV was amazingly durable, though early versions with the Renault carburetter were too thirsty, and despite the vast radiator boiling on long hills was not unknown. The 12·5:1 ratio of second gear was painfully low, Renault obstinately refusing to fit four speeds, while the engine's original 15 b.h.p. were never augmented to keep pace with increasing weight—except on a few sports versions (Type MT) with wire wheels and a higher axle ratio, which usually wore racy coachwork with 'cork in bottle' auxiliary seats in their long tails.

69 STONELEIGH 9 h.p.,
1922, Great Britain

The ordinary Armstrong Siddeley was truly a 'Car of Aircraft Quality', from its introduction in 1919 to its demise forty-one years later. Thus it comes as a surprise to find the company offering a near-cyclecar alongside their usual line of ponderous sixes. The Stoneleigh name, incidentally, had been used by the old Siddeley-Deasy concern for a B.S.A.-based sleeve-valve 13·9 h.p. car marketed in 1913–14.

The engine of the 1922 Stoneleigh also had some B.S.A. in its make-up,

being a vee-twin designed by Hotch-kiss of Coventry for B.S.A.'s 1921 light car, and taken over by that firm after W. R. Morris moved in. It was mounted in unit with a three-speed gearbox and drove to a differential-less back axle. The quarter-elliptic springs, disc wheels, and narrow-section tyres typified sub-utility motoring, though coil ignition was used. A starter was an optional extra, except on the last models of 1924, and the rearwards-hinged one-piece hood carried a dummy replica of Armstrong Siddeley's flat radiator, as used on their smaller and cheaper cars between 1924 and 1933.

The Stoneleigh's great eccentricity, however, lay in its cloverleaf seating, which reversed the usual idiom in that the driver sat centrally in solitary state. The rear seat was easily detachable to make room for luggage, and the bath-shaped body was fabricated from aluminium panels mounted on a wooden frame. It came in its natural finish, unpainted.

In the manner of its kind, the Stoneleigh was rough, noisy, and tricky to start from cold. Attempts were made to glamourise the ugly duckling with closed bodywork, which even included a little doctor's brougham, but nobody wanted the car, and one example, certainly, has survived because a disgruntled Armstrong Siddeley dealer took his demonstrator off the road with only a few hundred miles on the odometer. Only about 200 were made, and J. D. Siddeley never essayed another cheap lightweight. Indeed, his only subsequent small car, the Twelve Six of 1929, was the exact antithesis of the Stoneleigh: flexible, refined, easy to drive, and utterly gutless. Incredibly, in basic form it sold for little more than the £225 ($1,150) originally asked for the 1922 vee-twin.

70   O.M. 469, 1922, Italy

When Züst were acquired by the Officine Mecchaniche in 1918, the new owners revived the old 25–35 h.p. of 1913, but by 1920 this was being phased out in favour of a new model from the drawing-board of the Austrian Barratouché.

This had certain similarities with the 1½-litres made by FIAT, Ceirano, and Chiribiri, with a small and over-cooled side-valve four-cylinder engine, and low and wide gear ratios intended for assaults on the vertical. The monobloc unit featured a detachable head, an alloy crankcase, and a crankshaft running in three plain bearings, the thermosyphon circulation being assisted by a wood-bladed fan. The frame was a simple design with members of inverted U-section, though unusual for the period were the coil ignition and central ball change. The cars did well in local competitions, and as a consequence the original 1,327 c.c. Tipo-465 (four cylinders of 65 mm. bore) grew up first into the 467, and finally into the 1,496 c.c. 469. By this time Barratouché's Tipo-665 six had entered the picture, with the consequence that the four-cylinder O.M. continued virtually unaltered until 1930, though in the 1922–29 period magneto ignition was used. Starting was by Bosch dynamotor, and the carburetter was fed by Autovac from a ten-gallon rear tank.

Later fours had no sporting potential, though R. F. Oats of Rawlence's, the British concessionaires, tried to shift a stock of chassis on hand by some mild tuning, which eventually extracted a creditable 72 m.p.h. with open bodywork. For touring purposes, however, the O.M.'s 30 b.h.p. were quite adequate. From 1925 onwards the chassis was used for a range of light commercial vehicles (Tipo 469F).

In 1930 the company decided to concentrate on trucks, but the 469, now with a bigger, 1,680 c.c. engine, soldiered on into 1934, and was actually displayed at the 1933 Milan Show. Most of these later models were, however, vans or taxis, and after 1931 O.M.'s passenger-car operations were limited to the sale of stockpiled chassis, organised by the Esperia firm formed by two O. M. executives.

71   DOBLE E-13, 1923, U.S.A.

The E- and F-series Dobles of 1923–32 represented the ultimate in steam-car design. All the old snags had been eliminated. Firing up from cold, which before had taken at least 25 minutes, was now a matter of 45 seconds. Controls had been simplified: a driver unfamiliar with the Doble would not be confronted with a plethora of steam cocks. Instead he would notice the absence of a gear lever, and possibly the special pressure cap on the big 'radiator'. What is more, the traditional virtues of steam were still present. Direct drive meant complete flexibility, and a Doble would waft its way silently up to its maximum speed of

85 m.p.h., yet trickle through traffic at a crawl. The efficient condensing system allowed of a continuous cruising speed of 70 m.p.h., and frequent stops for water were unnecessary.

As early as 1912 Abner Doble had demonstrated his Model-A roadster to the Stanley brothers. This car offered 75 m.p.h., an 0–60 m.p.h. acceleration time of 15 seconds, and a range between refills of 1,000 miles, though it never reached production. The 1917 Doble-Detroit, a war casualty, represented another step forward, for Doble dispensed with the old-type burner, and its need for a bi-fuel system. Instead he resorted to electric firing, by means of a sparking plug in the base of the combustion chamber, at the mouth of the venturi.

Model-E was, however, a super-car by any standards, costing $8,000 in open form and as much as $12,000 (£2,400) with closed bodywork: all bodies were made by Murphy of Pasadena. The engine, a four-cylinder, double-acting cross-compound, lived on the rear axle, where it was automatically lubricated at 500-mile intervals, and the crankcase was integral with the axle casing. The monotube boiler, working at a pressure of 750 psi, was mounted under the bonnet with its electric burner, and refinements included a steering wheel of African ebony with a spider made of German silver. On 125 b.h.p., the car was more powerful than its petrol-engined contemporaries, while Dobles were guaranteed for 100,000 miles. The high price and Doble's inability to gain adequate financial backing resulted in the breed's demise after less than fifty cars had been made.

72   NASH FOUR, 1922, 1923, U.S.A.

Charles W. Nash, a former vice-president of General Motors, took over the old-established Jeffery concern in 1917, and for the next forty years the cars bearing his name sold steadily, if never spectacularly. Nash's highest placing in the American best-seller league between the wars was eighth (in 1921, 1928, and 1929) and their record production figure for the period a mere 138,000 cars in 1928.

Like the other independents, however, Nash were not afraid to break new ground, and in an age of stereotyped thinking they were staunch adherents of pushrod-operated o.h.v. which still featured on their more expensive models in 1942, having been introduced on the first Nash Six of 1917. Other innovations were air conditioning (1938) and unitary construction (1941).

The four-cylinder was announced as an inexpensive companion for the Six in 1921. Its valve gear and transmission handbrake apart, it displayed no deviations from the American norm. Lubrication was by splash, a 6-volt coil took care of the ignition, and fuel feed was by vacuum, while there were three forward speeds, a plate clutch, and a spiral bevel back axle. List price of a touring car was $1,395 (£279), reduced to $985 a year later; some of the closed models were not unattractive. The 1923 catalogue contained something called a 'carriole', which was really an answer to Essex's coach beautified by the addition of a small trunk with ribbed bars. This accessory, incidentally, was furnished by other American manufacturers as part of that group of extras known as 'sport equipment'.

Like Hudson, however, Nash fell for the blandishments of cheap multi-cylinderism, and in 1925 the Four gave way to an ordinary side-valve six which, in the manner of the times, its makers preferred to market under the brand-name of Ajax. It lasted only a couple of seasons, though it left its mark. Thereafter the cheaper Nash models invariably had L-head engines, and the lineal descendant of the Ajax unit eventually found its way into Nash's most successful car, the compact Rambler of 1950.

73 CITROËN 5CV, 1923, France

Unkind critics have asserted that the 5CV Citroën neither went nor stopped. Certainly it lacked front-wheel brakes even in 1926, and only on the last of the line was the brake pedal coupled to the drums on the rear wheels as well as to the transmission. 38 m.p.h. was its accepted maximum speed, but the proof of the pudding is in the eating, and about 80,000 5CVs were sold, not to mention the numerous direct copies made in Germany by Opel. Its demise was so lamented in France that in 1929 Emile Dombrey endeavoured to market a modernised edition, the Sima-Standard. This was a curious hotchpotch of Citroën and Amilcar parts, but it lasted for four seasons, while until very recent times aged cloverleafs have been a common sight in rural France.

Designed by Jules Salomon, who had already been responsible for the 10CV of 1919, the Citroën was a simple little car. Cooling was by thermo-syphon,

ignition was by coil, the dynamo was driven directly off the nose of the crankshaft, and an electric starter was standard, even in 1921. The channel-section frame rode on quarter-elliptic springs; shock absorbers were not provided. The wheels were Michelin discs, and weight was 952 pounds. Initially it was offered only as a pointed-tail two-seater, finished in lemon yellow with black wings, and by 1922 it was selling in England for £195 ($980), a price which explains how Citroën managed to dispose of 3,000 cars in the United Kingdom during 1923.

Like the 6CV Renault, the Citroën was steadily improved, though it also acquired a few more brake horses, alloy pistons being standardised in 1923, when magneto ignition was also adopted, and the wheelbase was lengthened to accommodate the three-seater cloverleaf body. A neat little cabriolet was also offered. 1924 saw the advent of low-pressure tyres and a five-lamp lighting set. Proprietary firms took matters further, offering o.h.v. and front-wheel brake conversions, but in 1926 Citroën decided to concentrate all their efforts on the 10CV category, and though this one-model policy did not last long, they were not destined to cater for the minimal motorist again until 1949, when the revolutionary *deux chevaux* was unveiled.

74 LEYAT, 1923, France

France has always been the home of the bizarre, but Marcel Leyat's airscrew-driven automobile (and its contemporary, the Traction Aérienne) were perhaps the oddest of all motorcars to see series production. A photograph of Leyat's shops taken in 1921 actually shows three different examples parked side-by-side.

Leyat had worked for the Astra aeronautical company before setting up on his own, and his ideas embraced an aeroplane without wings. The unitary-construction fuselage carried its motor in the nose, driving a tractor propeller which was protected by a wire-mesh guard within a ring of wood or steel. There was, of course, no gearbox, controls being limited to a cable-starter, an ignition switch, a throttle and a decompressor.

Alarmingly, however, Leyat had opted for front-wheel brakes, with separate pedals for each wheel, and rear-wheel steering *via* a cable-and-bobbin linkage. A lock on the right-hand pedal did duty as a handbrake, and the inventor insisted that these curious arrangements rendered his cars skid-proof. Various engines were tried, among them a British A.B.C. flat-twin with twin carburetters, and a three-cylinder Anzani radial, while both open and closed 'bodies' were available, the former having tandem cockpits in the best light-aeroplane tradition. Weight of open models came out at 510 pounds, the 'sedans' being slightly heavier at 624 pounds, though the Leyat, with its 1,200 c.c. engine, did not of course qualify as a cyclecar. This was perhaps as well, as it could hardly have conformed with any racing regulations then in force!

The factory claimed 50 m.p.h. and 48 m.p.g. for their early models, but one of their creations achieved over 100 m.p.h. at Montlhéry Autodrome,

and in 1921 some brave soul drove a Leyat from Paris to Bordeaux in 12 hours, despite appalling road conditions. Alas, for M. Leyat, he was a voice crying in the wilderness, and few Frenchmen were willing to expend 11,500 francs on a wingless aeroplane.

75 ZEDEL 11CV, 1923,
France

The Zedel was another of those stolid, orthodox motor cars which proliferated in France during the early 1920s. Even its cylinder dimensions were common to a variety of models.

The name derived from the partnership formed in 1899 by two Swiss engineers, Ernst Zurcher and Hermann Luthi. Zurcher had already been responsible for Switzerland's first motorcycle power unit, and the firm established itself in a new works at St. Aubin, where they manufactured proprietary units on a scale almost comparable with that of Minerva or de Dion. Light cars followed, and in 1905 a branch factory was set up on the French side of the border at Pontarlier to make these: in fact the cars soon assumed French nationality, while additional factory space was found near Paris at Nanterre. In 1914 the standard models were a 2-litre 9CV and a 2·1-litre 11CV, both with four-cylinder engines.

1921, however, saw a new owner in the shape of Jérome Donnet. Donnet, like Emile Mathis, aspired to volume production. In 1924 the company made over two thousand cars, albeit they were still wedded to developments of their pre-War themes. By the end of the year, however, the first of a new generation was available. The 1,100 c.c. side-valve four-cylinder 7CV boasted a four-speed gearbox, and this light car was followed by a 2½-litre six of American aspect, designed by Sainturat. Some smaller sixes ensued, while Donnet also experimented with a Violet-designed two-stroke twin, the 4CV 'Donette' of 1932, with front-wheel drive, and ultimately with all-independent suspension. The company collapsed in 1934, the Nanterre works being acquired by H. T. Pigozzi's Simca concern for the licence-production of FIATs.

76 NAPIER 40–50 h.p.,
1923, Great Britain

Thanks to their great propagandist, S. F. Edge, Napier, the pioneers of the six-cylinder engine, could still be mentioned in the same breath as Rolls-Royce, even in 1910. Admittedly they offered too many models; not every owner of a lordly Sixty liked to see the same water-tower radiator cap on two-cylinder taxis chugging around London's clubland. Edge departed in 1913, and before the War was over the ailing Montague Napier had decided to concentrate his efforts on aero-engines.

Thus the Rowledge-designed T.75 was a deliberate swansong. On the surface it belonged to the new generation, with its light alloy block and pistons, detachable head, shrunk-in steel liners, and vertical shaft-driven overhead camshaft. The S.U. carburetter incorporated an auxiliary instrument for slow running, ignition was by Watford magneto and C.A.V.

coil, and the under-bonnet scene was more attractive than the Rolls-Royce's untidy landscape. The four-speed gearbox had central change, the standard top-gear ratio was 3·33 to 1, and the Napier came in two wheelbase lengths, 137 and 144 inches. Early reports spoke of 65–70 m.p.h. and 13–16 m.p.g., and a tourer submitted to a long Alpine work-out in 1921 gave no trouble at all—apart from having to reverse on 25 of the Stelvio Pass's 44 hairpins.

Unfortunately there were snags. The Napier was noisier than the Rolls-Royce, yet lacked the superb brakes and handling of the Hispano-Suiza. The foot transmission brake was fade-prone, and the high-geared steering was heavy at low speeds. While Rolls-Royce sold chassis only, Napier had a 'tame' coachbuilder, Cunard, and Cunard's efforts were sometimes lacking in elegance. An embarrassing engine 'period' was only cured by using a concave crown in number six piston to reduce the compression. Finally, the 40–50 took an unconscionable time to reach the public: it was exhibited at the 1919 London Show, but no chassis were ready for the coachbuilders until June, 1920, and then a strike at Cunard's caused further delays. Eventually 187 of the last Napier model were produced, four-wheel brakes being adopted in 1924, but that year saw the end of a distinguished line.

77 TROJAN PB, 1923,
Great Britain

Leyland's two private-car ventures have been summarised as 'dignity and impudence', and when the Lancashire company undertook the manufacture of Leslie Hounsfield's two-stroke utility car at Kingston, Parry Thomas wrote an indignant disclaimer to the motoring press.

Hounsfield had been experimenting with utility transport since 1910, and to the end he remained faithful to the two-stroke engine, as well as eschewing a conventional location for it. On his pre-1914 prototype it lived vertically between the seats, between 1923 and 1929 it was mounted under the floor, and on the final RE series (1930–36) it was perched over the rear axle, driving forward by chain.

The definitive Trojan (about 15,000 were made) was the Leyland-built model. It used a 1½-litre monobloc square-four engine with only seven moving parts, lubricated by petroil, and set horizontally under the seats in a punt-type chassis. The transmission consisted of a two-speed-and-reverse epicyclic gear, drive being transmitted by duplex roller chain to a live rear axle: there was no differential. The cantilever suspension gave an excellent ride, this enabling Hounsfield to economise by fitting solid tyres as standard, which saved about £4 per car, as well as reducing running costs.

Nor did this end a catalogue of eccentricity. The conventional bonnet was empty save for the carburetter and fuel tank, though the radiator was real. There was neither electric starter nor conventional starting handle; one energised a Trojan *via* a pull-up handle in the cockpit.

If the top speed of 34 m.p.h. was uncomfortable on solids (pneumatics cost £5 extra), an amazingly flat power curve enabled the engine to deliver almost all its eleven brake horses at any rate of rotation from 450 r.p.m. up to the maximum of 1,200: it would therefore ascend the vertical, albeit at a snail's pace. Top gear would cope with a 1-in-9 gradient. Decarbonising was unnecessary, and 100,000-mile intervals between major overhauls were not uncommon. If many Britons considered the Trojan too unconventional and uncouth for a passenger car, commercial operators did not share their squeamishness, and among those who ran large fleets of Trojan vans were the R.A.F., Brooke Bond Tea, and Post Office Telephones. Understandably, the company elected to concentrate production—which had been on a modest scale since the divorce with Leyland—on light commericals after 1936.

78 AUDI K 14/50 PS, 1923, Germany

The Audi company had been formed by Dr. August Horch after a disagreement with his board in 1909. Barred from using his name on a second make of car, he quietly rendered it into Latin, thus disarming his opponents; but either way the result was a better Horch, retaining the overhead inlet valves he had long favoured. His 3½-litre *Alpensieger* deserved its name, winning the team prize in the 1913 Austrian Alpine Trials, and dead-heating with Hansa in 1914.

Horch himself resigned in 1920, leaving technical development in the hands of Lange, who had a replacement for the old pre-War types ready by 1922. The 3½-litre engine had pushrod-operated overhead valves, and the basic specification contained no outstanding heresies. What was interesting was the widespread use of light alloys, for block, pistons, and axle casing. A positive gear-change was assured by attaching the central lever direct to the four-speed box, Rudge wire wheels were standard, and unusual features were the gearbox-driven tyre pump and the folding 'fat man's' steering wheel. It was also the first German car to come with left-hand drive as standard, and though a transmission brake was retained, the pedal now worked in drums on the rear wheels. Top speed was about 60 m.p.h., but the big 14/50 had only a short run, being withdrawn at the end of 1924 in favour of the 18/70 PS Model-M, a disastrous step for a small and poor firm. A 4·7-litre six-cylinder overhead-camshaft engine was lubricated by no fewer than three oil pumps, and there were also one-shot chassis lubrication and servo-assisted hydraulic brakes on all four wheels. It was handsome and it was capable of 80 m.p.h., but it was impossibly expensive to make, and a chassis price of 24,000 marks (about £1,200) put in into direct competition with such monsters as the six-cylinder supercharged Mercedes and the W2 Maybach. It is not surprising that after 1927 J. S. Rasmussen, Audi's new owner, concentrated on a line of s.v. straight-eights in the American idiom, using the factory largely for the construction of bodies for his utility two-stroke D.K.W.s.

79 FIAT 501, 1923, Italy

Ever since the Agadir Crisis of 1907, FIAT had been moving steadily towards the role of General Provider for Europe, and not just to foreign plutocracy at large. The original s.v. monobloc *Tipo* 1 of 1908 had evolved by 1912 into the 1·8-litre *Tipo* Zero, capable of 50 m.p.h., and retailing for under £400 ($2,000) in England. During the War Carlo Cavalli went to work on a new family of FIATs with side-valve engines, detachable heads, full electrics, and all brakes on the rear wheels. His transitional model, the 2-litre *Tipo* 70, was ready by 1916 and went into limited production during the last two years of hostilities.

The 1½-litre 501 represented the smallest family car that Cavalli considered viable for international markets. Output of the simple three-bearing engine was 21–22 b.h.p. at 2,600 r.p.m., ignition was by magneto, and the unit was cooled (over-cooled would be more exact) by pump and fan. Both the four-speed unit gearbox and the multi-plate clutch were sweet in action, though ratios were low and wide, a 25 to 1 bottom gear emphasising the vehicle's near-Alpine origins. The rear-wheel brakes were indifferent, and the model excelled neither in acceleration nor in straight-line speed; even touring cars weighed close on a ton, and 50 m.p.h. was about the limit. Where the car scored was in its smoothness, silence, and astonishing durability: survivors are to be found in almost every country of the world. Little was done to the design during its long run (1919–26), though the ugly 'military fenders' of early models gave way to the crown type during 1922 and in 1924 balloon tyres and four-wheel brakes became optional extras. Total production amounted to close on 80,000 cars.

Variations on the theme were limitless. There was a sports version, the 501S, in 1921; this had a 26 b.h.p. engine and would exceed 60 m.p.h. with the aid of a 4·6 to 1 back axle, though Italian tuners made it go much faster, Silvani claiming 89 m.p.h. from his fiercest o.h.v. conversion. The twin o.h.c. 501SS (a racing *voiturette* engine in a 501S chassis) was never on general sale, but for export there was a 'colonial' version with wider track and lightened chassis, and from 1923 onwards hire-car operators were given a long-chassis edition, the 502, which could carry six-seater bodywork.

80 LILA, 1923, Japan

Japan was slow to develop a motor industry. Her roads were narrow and tortuous, and government-sponsored Automobile Control Laws laid down what could be made and what could not, overall dimensions being restricted as well as cylinder capacity, which explains why the first Datson of 1931 had a narrow track of only 39 inches. Thus the best customer for any would-be manufacturer with aspirations outside the cyclecar class was the Government, who wanted American-type vehicles, and bought them from the native industry as well as from Detroit's Japanese assembly plants (both Ford and Chevrolet were assembling there by 1925). Some makers copied European designs, as witness Ishikawajima's Wolseleys, and the twenty Type-A Mitsubishis made in 1917–19, which were FIATs in all but name. By contrast, Junya Toyokawa's Hakuyosha Ironworks of Tokyo managed to turn out some 270 Otomo light cars with air- and water-cooled four-cylinder engines in the middle 1920s.

The real father of the Japanese automobile industry was, however, an American aircraft engineer named William R. Gorham who settled in Japan and became a Japanese citizen. Gorham's Jitsuyo Jidosha Seizo Company entered the automobile industry when he designed a three-wheeled invalid tricar for his works manager. This curious little vehicle had handle-bar steering, and an air-cooled twin-cylinder engine drove the right rear wheel, but the Gorham's compact proportions proved admirably suited to the narrow Japanese roads, and a fair number of the cars were produced: they can be regarded as the direct ancestors of Japan's commercial three-wheelers, which were popular until the very late 1960s, among the leading manufacturers being Daihatsu and Mazda. A bigger shaft-driven four-wheeler followed, this evolving into the Lila of 1923, which was made for three seasons in passenger and commercial forms. Its air-cooled 10 h.p. engine gave it a top speed of 30 m.p.h. In 1926 J.J.S. merged with Kwaishinsha (Dat), and the combined group elected to concentrate on trucks until 1930, when a change of policy resulted in the 500 c.c. four-cylinder Datson (Son of Dat) which later became the Datsun. By 1938 the resultant Nissen Motor Co. was said to be capable of turning out 18,000 passenger cars a year, though Japan's military expansionism probably diverted most of these to the Imperial armed forces.

INDEX

Make	Model	Ref. No. (colour)	Page No. (description)
Standard	9·5 h.p.	11	104
Star	11·9 h.p.	58	137
Stoneleigh	9 h.p.	69	145
Swift	7·9 h.p.	12	104
Templar	1922	64	141
Trojan	PB	77	150
Trumbull	1914	20	110
Vermorel	12CV	6	100
Voisin	C4	56	136
Wanderer	5/12 PS, 5/15 PS	26	114
Wills–Sainte Claire	1922	65	142
Woods Mobilette	1914, 1915	3	98
Zedel	11CV	75	149
Zust	25–35 h.p.	14	106